1495

POEMS OF PIERRE DE RONSARD

POEMS OF PIERRE DE RONSARD

translated and edited,
with Introduction and Notes,
by
Nicholas Kilmer

UNIVERSITY OF CALIFORNIA PRESS
Berkeley   Los Angeles   London

University of California Press
Berkeley and Los Angeles, California

University of California Press, Ltd.
London, England

ISBN 0-520-03078-8
Library of Congress Catalog Card Number: 75-17287
Copyright © 1979 by The Regents of the University of California

Printed in the United States of America

The translations of *Le Voyage de Tours* and *Folastrie* first appeared in ARION, New Series, Vol. 3, Numbers 2 and 3, 1976, and are reprinted with the kind permission of the Trustees of Boston University.

This book is designed and decorated by Nicholas Kilmer.

Julia,

    When I came to my room to make this book, I found
    Stretched towels covered the floor and chairs. The leaves
    Of lemon balm and sage, rosemary, mint; the petals
    Of roses of all colors spread to dry here, made
    Such fragrance I was ashamed
    My occupation had no color in it, nor any
    Method by which a room might be made welcome.

    We must advise each other with these thin dry skins,
    And love them, and ourselves be thin and dry
    So that our fragrances survive to make some places fond after we die.

CONTENTS

INTRODUCTION

The large amount of work he left us, its versatility, and its evenness of competence, show Ronsard to have been a poet who learned to make his art a necessary part of his daily life—even to the point that he did his dying in poetry.

I have assembled here a series of poems that will allow the few small poems for which Ronsard is well known to be seen within the context of his intellectual development. In the notes I have added what seemed to me necessary to explain the values of those elements of Ronsard's world which appear in his poems as images.

Ronsard is a metaphysical poet, a manipulator and transformer. His perception operates by metaphor. His poems are a record of his thinking, a visual process that is represented by a series of images translated into words.

The logic of the visual thinker can be distracting. The shift from one image to another can be sudden, seem illogical, because it proceeds by analogical principles that are visual rather than verbal. Further, it is normal for different kinds of vision (the immediate, the remembered, the invented or pretended, the composite, the accidental, the unconscious), to operate interchangeably.

Much of Ronsard's poetry originates in a metaphysical premise which affirms an interchangeability of matter. The impermanence of material forms makes itself felt through the variability of appearances. This premise also contains the theme of the disintegration that is the central passage in the process of transformation. This is not purely abstract principle, but a record of the mode in which Ronsard perceived and experienced the world.

Within such a world the substantial integrity of the human appears desperately fragile. The nature of the human, during the time when the matter that makes it up can be called human, needs to be described, and in some way confirmed by the witness of experience and by the legacy of a permanent record.

The love poems are the only *ergo* that can follow the premise of the transitory nature of the human: ergo that is both conclusion and argument: we must take notice that we are for this instant complementary arrangements; and we should celebrate that.

Ronsard lived in a country ravaged by civil and religious wars and persecutions, by plague and famine. The form of Renaissance Christianity was a dualistic one, in which matter was seen as deriving its value from the infusion of spirit, which was either God or something like God; and the human body was in turn made valuable only by the presence in it of God's image, which was the human soul. Matter without soul, if conceivable, was despicable. However, one had to avoid the charge of pantheism which might accompany the assignment of too great a spiritual presence within the everyday world.

It was the value of this visible everyday world that Ronsard defended. His defense consisted in affirming the metaphysical principles that seemed to make the world humane and sensible; recording the usefulness and variety of its elements; making permanent those things and moments that were so transitory as otherwise to appear to be illusory.

It was not beauty or order that made value in Ronsard's world, but realness, usefulness, the practical applicability objects have to one another. Ronsard loved knowing the names for different parts of the plow; he loved knowing how wine was made, and who performed which labors in the process. He loved knowing the names, the shapes, and the medical values of plants, and where to find them. Most of all he loved what he spoke last of leaving: houses, orchards, gardens. It was here finally that the human presence in the world was noted as beneficial. This shaping human presence was what made Ronsard's world worth remarking and preserving.

Ovid blessed his world by claiming its wilder places to be inhabited by spirits of woods and water. Ronsard claimed the same right, because he would not willingly forgo the blessings left him as inheritance. But he was more content to speak of the tamed French countryside; to point to things growing around him and know that

Virgil, Ovid, Hesiod had known these things; that they were his now, and belonged to his language; that they were his to make provision for. Ronsard wished to leave a testament that might provide for those who would follow him in a thousand years (that is six hundred years from now) evidence of a reasonable, comprehensive, humane arrangement that was not only a gathering of inherited knowledge and custom but an interpretation of it as well.

A small but important part of that legacy concerns Ronsard's intimate awareness of himself, the realness of his own emotional nature: its dependence, independence, and variability. His poems show him to be a man of brilliant and subtle humor, intense, passionate, bitter at times, and always graceful.

A poem is designed for efficiency. Its form is a matter of courtesy. Politeness, tact, diplomacy change as rapidly as do all other human customs.

The translator of Ronsard must reckon not only with a change of language but also with a change of manners, between sixteenth-century France and twentieth-century America.

My interest has been to make these versions an adequate witness to the nature of Ronsard's thinking. I have not taken an imitation of sixteenth-century French manners to be an essential part of that task; though I have felt obliged to imitate Ronsard's care, and to see to it that my versions be acceptable poems—that is, that they be efficient, courteous, and carefully made.

Those who have been familiar with Ronsard's poems in French may find themselves surprised that what is presented here does not always attempt to sound like Ronsard's poems. My versions will not tend to rhyme at the ends of lines. They will not necessarily match Ronsard's in the number of their lines. Where I have chosen to use a regular meter (rather frequently in the longer, more conversational and discursive poems, and in cases where the meter expects to be applied to singing, or makes a joke), it is not necessarily the meter that Ronsard uses himself.

Rhetoric is one element of diplomacy, a formal arrangement that changes as easily as other customs do. Certain mechanical rhetorical devices—that of personification for example—were convincing forms for argument in Ronsard's day, but will no longer serve in ours, and I have felt it best to find other devices to take their places. In some instances, where I felt that my solution might be surprising to some readers, I have used the notes to give an indication of the kind of thinking that produced it.

In general, since Ronsard's logic is metaphoric, those of his poems that depend on logic (the sonnets particularly) are interweavings of visual evidence and abstract theory. He himself tends to begin with his visual argument and proceed to the abstract. I find it occasionally more telling to reverse this order, beginning with the abstract and working toward the visible.

It is for this reason that in my version of *Comme on voit* (42 in this selection) I take Ronsard's final line and place it at the beginning. Ronsard's poem announces a person's death, and makes it credible, and shocking. It announces an intimacy between the dead and the living, and makes that intimacy credible. It makes an old and much used comparison (the rose will die: you will die) credible and, since it is credible, moving. It makes your body roses. I feel obliged to bring about the same results by whatever means seem adequately efficient, courteous, and technically sound.

My poems will be at times more vivid than Ronsard's; more elliptical; more surprising. In part that may be because my poems must function in a culture that is less patient with poetry. Perhaps more to the point, Ronsard is speaking to people who are familiar with the world to which his images refer. My versions speak to people (myself included) for whom that world has become largely invisible, and I may hope that a certain increase in vividness can make up for our lack of habituation. In the long run, I trust that Ronsard's careful balance between vision and logic has been honored in my practice, and maintained; that his careful music has been answered, if not echoed.

1. A CHARLES DE PISSELEU
EVESQUE DE CONDON

L'honneur sans plus du verd laurier m'agrée,
  Par lui je hai le vulgaire odieus,
  Voila pour quoi Euterpe la sacrée
  M'a de mortel fait compagnon des Dieus.

Aussi el' m'aime, & par les bois m'amuse,
  Me tient, m'embrasse, & quand je veil sonner,
  De m'accorder ses fleutes ne refuse
  Ne de m'apprendre à bien les entonner.

Car elle m'a de l'eau de ses fontaines
  Pour prestre sien baptisé de sa main,
  Me faisant part du haut honneur d'Athenes,
  Et du sçavoir de l'antique Romain.

I have become the gods' mortal companion.
Euterpe, the most holy muse of verse, has made this of me;
And I may now despise common pretenders,
Content with the honor of the green laurel wreath.

And the Muse loves me, entertains me. Amongst woods
She hugs and holds me. When I want to make music
She loans her flutes.

When I was young she plunged me in her fountain
With her own hand, baptized me to her priesthood:
Making me part of high Athens' glory,
Part of the ancient wisdom of the Romans.

2. A LA FORÊT DE GASTINE

Couché sous tes umbrages vers
  Gastine je te chante
Autant que les Grecs par leurs vers
  La forest d'Erymanthe,

Car malin, celer je ne puis
  A la race future,
De combien obligé je suis
  A ta belle verdure.

Toi, qui sous l'abri de tes bois,
  Ravi d'esprit m'amuses,
Toi, qui fais qu'à toutes les fois
  Me répondent les Muses.

Toi, par qui de ce mechant soin
  Tout franc je me delivre,
Lors qu'en toi je me pers bien loin,
  Parlant avec un livre.

Tes bocages soient toujours pleins
  D'Amoureuses brigades,
De Satyres & de Sylvains,
  La crainte des Naiades.

En toi habite desormais
  Des Muses le college,
Et ton bois ne sente jamais
  La flamme sacrilege.

I sing you, Gastine,
Couched under your green shadows.
Greeks made into song
The woods of Erymanthus.

I could not be so sly
I'd hide from those who follow
How deep my obligation
To your lovely leafage.

Your trees' shelter
Delights my amazed mind.
You cause the muses to answer me.

You have delivered me frankly
From all commotions,
Because I disappear amongst you
And converse with my books.

Let your thickets be filled always
With amorous troops
Of Nymphs. May goatfoot fauns
Terrorize Naiads.

The college of the Muses
Will live here hereafter,
And your wood not scent
The flame of sacrilege.

3. A CUPIDON

Le jour pousse la nuit,
    Et la nuit sombre
Pousse le jour qui luit
    D'une obscure ombre.

L'autumne suit l'esté,
    Et l'âpre rage
Des vens, n'a point été
    Apres l'orage.

Mais le mal nonobstant
    D'amour dolente,
Demeure en moi constant
    Et ne s'alente.

Ce n'estoit pas nous, Dieu,
    Qui failloit poindre,
Ta fleche en autre lieu
    Se devoit joindre.

Poursui les paresseus
    Et les amuse,
Mais non pas moi, ne ceus
    Qu'aime la Muse.

Day thrusts the night
And then black night
Thrusts out the day to burn
Through her black shadow.

Fall chases summer,
And the harsh raging of wind
Falls after storm.

But the pain
Of love's grieving
Stays constant in me
And will not falter.

It is not me, Lord,
Whom you need pierce;
But let your arrow aim
Toward other targets.

Take on some lazy folks
Who need amusement:
But let me be,
And those who love the Muse.

4. DE LA VENUE DE L'ESTÉ

AU SEIGNEUR DE BONNIVET EVESQUE DE BESIERS

ODE X

Ja-ja, les grans chaleurs s'émeuvent,
  Et presque les fleuves ne peuvent
  Leurs peuples escaillés couvrir,
  Ja voit on la plaine alterée
  Par la grande torche aithérée
  De soif se lâcher, & s'ouvrir.

L'estincelante Canicule,
  Qui ard, qui cuist, qui boust, qui brule,
  L'esté nous darde de là haut,
  Et le souleil qui se promeine
  Par les braz du Cancre, rameine
  Ces mois tant pourboullis du chaut.

Ici, la diligente troupe
  Des ménagers renverse, & coupe
  Le poil de Ceres jaunissant,
  Et là, jusques à la vesprée
  Abbat les honneurs de la prée,
  Des beaus prez l'honneur verdissant.

Ce pendant leurs femmes sont prestes
  D'assurer au haut de leurs testes
  Des plats de bois, ou des baris,
  Et fillant, marchent par la plaine
  Pour aller apâter le peine
  De leurs laborieus maris.

Si tost ne s'esveille l'Aurore,
  Que le pasteur ne soit encore
  Plustost levé qu'elle, & allors
  Au son de la corne reveille
  Son troupeau qui encor sommeille
  Desus la fresche herbe dehors.

for Ron and Ellen Story

The great heats are already on us.
Rivers barely cover their fishes' fins.
Flat country, altered
By fiery wind,
Slackens and cracks with thirst.

The dog star glints its eye,
Gleams, glows, roasts, broils.
Summer glares from the sky
And the sun promenades at Cancer's elbow
Gathering her flock of heat-browned months.

A crowd of laborers cuts
In careful ranks,
The yellowed bristling fur from Ceres' skin
And still into the evening
Strips down the trophies from the fields,
The green pride from the lovely fields.

The women bustle, balancing
Wood platters, casks of wine on their heads;
And pass among the fields;
Comfort their husbands' thirsty labors.

Before the morning
Star rises, the shepherd wakes
His flock, still sleeping in cold grasses,
With his horn's shrill.

Amongst the uncovered fields,
The woods, the green stream banks,
The cattle browse, or gallop
Through flowers that Apollo takes,
Or those born from Adonis' blood.

Parmi les plaines découvertes,
  Par les bois, & les rives vertes,
  Paist le bestail, plustost courant
  Entre les fleurs Apollinées,
  Ou entre celles du sang nées
  Du bel Adonis, en mourant.

Au long des flancs des belles ondes
  Les jeunes troupes vagabondes,
  Les filles des troupeaus lacifs
  De fronts retournés s'entrechocquent,
  Devant leurs peres qui s'en mocquent
  Au haut du prochain tertre assis.

Mais quand en sa distance egale
  Est le souleil, & la cigale
  Epand l'enroué de sa vois,
  Et que nul Zephire n'alceine
  Tant soit peu les fleurs en la pleine,
  Ne la teste ombreuse des bois,

Adonc le pasteur entrelasse
  Ses paniers de torse pelasse,
  Ou il englue les oiseaux,
  Ou nu comme un poisson il noue,
  Et avec les ondes se joue
  Cherchant tousjours le fond des eaus.

Si l'antique fable est croiable,
  Erigone la pitoiable
  En tels mois alla luire aus cieus,
  En forme de vierge, qui ores
  Reçoit dedans son sein encores
  Le commun œil de tous les dieus:

Œil inconnu de nos valées,
  Où les fonteines devalées
  Du vif rocher vont murmurant,
  Et où mile troupeaus se pressent,
  Et le nés contre terre bessent
  Si grande chaleur endurant.

Along the sliding flanks of streams
The urgent yearling she-goats
Jostle and toss before the fathering bucks
Who mock them, lordly on neighboring hillocks.

When the sun floats at noon
The cricket floods its strident creaking.
Not a breath tilts the smallest flower
Nor the trees' shadowy heads.

The shepherd weaves his baskets of twisted withes,
Snares birds,
Or naked as a fish he swims
And plays with waves
Hunting the deepest water.

If the old story can be credited,
Erigone, whom we may pity,
Hangs shining in the sky
A starry virgin; in these months
Takes to her lap
The common eye of all the gods.

An eye our valleys do not know,
Where the springs leaping down
From live rock, make their murmurings,
And milling herds hasten,
Nuzzling the earth,
Their sides heaving with heat.

In cool oak shadow
The drowsy cows chew on their cuds
To the piteous constant bawl
Of the star crossed heifer whose ungrateful lover
Bull, ramps in the woods.

The herder, baffled,
Attempts to blow his pipes
To cool his wound: and keeps at it
Till Phoebus rides on the horizon,
Plunges his chariot in the western ocean:

Sous les chênes qui refrechissent,
Remaschent les beufs qui languissent
Au piteus cri continuel
De la genisse qui lamente
L'ingrate amour dont la tourmente
Son mari felon & cruel.

Lors le pasteur qui s'en estonne,
S'essaie du flageol qui sonne.
Amenuiser son accident,
Ce qu'il fait, tant qu'il voie pendre
Contre bas Phebus, & desçendre
Son chariot en l'Occident.

Puis de toutes pars il r'assemble
Sa troupe vagabonde ensemble,
Et la convoie aus douces eaus,
Qui sobre en les beuvant ne touche
Sans plus que du haut de la bouche
Le premier front des pleins ruisseaux.

Adonc au son de ses musettes,
Marchent les troupes camusettes
Pour aller trouver le sejour,
Où les aspres chaleurs deçoivent
Par un dormir qu'elles reçoivent
Lentement jusque au point du jour.

Then draws together
His vagrant troops
And brings them to sweet water
Where they drink slowly
Touching their lips only
To the filled stream brims.

The evening hums with piping;
The flocks of sheep
Amble toward sleep
Where no heat finds them,
Where they gently rest till dawn.

5. A DIEU POUR LA FAMINE

O Dieu des exercites,
  Qui aus Israëlites
Donnant jadis secours,
Fendis en deus le cours
De la rouge eau salée,
Et comme une valée
Que deus tertres épars
Emmurent de deus pars,
Tu fis au milieu d'elle
Une voie fidelle,
Où à pié sec parmi
Passa ton peuple ami.
Et puis en renversant
Le flot obeissant
Sus le Prince obstiné,
Tu as exterminé
Lui, & sa gent noiée
Sous l'onde renvoiée.
Ton peuple errant de là
Aus desers çà & là,
Les veaus de fonte adore,
Mais pour sa faute encore
Le ciel ne laissa pas
De pleuvoir son repas,
Qu'il receut de ta grace
Par quarante ans d'espace.
O Seigneur, retourne ores
Tes yeus, & voi encores
Ton peuple languissant,
Ton peuple perissant,
Que la palle famine
(Mort étrange) extermine.

You are the God of hosts;
And you once gave your aid
To Israel's escape.
You cleft into two parts
The course of red salt water;
Like valley stretched it out
Between two distant knolls
That walled it on both sides.
And in the midst of that
You made trustworthy road,
Through which, their feet dry, moved
The people whom you loved.
And then you flooded in
Your own obedient wave
Over the headstrong king,
Exterminating him
And all his drowning race.
Cast up safe from this sea
Your people wandered then
In deserts back and forth;
Adored the casted calf.
But even for that sin
Heaven did not refrain
From sending food like rain:
Which they had in that place
Forty years by your grace.
Oh Master, turn again
Your eyes, and look on us,
Your people sickening,
Your people perishing;
Because this foreign death
Pale famine, kills us all.

Pere, nous sçavons bien
Selon tes lois, combien
Nos journalieres fautes
Sont horribles & hautes:
Et voiant nos pechés
Dont sommes entachés,
Que ceste affliction
N'est pas punition:
Mais nous sçavons aussi,
Que nous aurons merci
Toutes les fois que nous
Flechissans les genous
Et soulevans la face
Demanderons ta grace.
Lâs, ô Dieu, sur nous veille,
Et de benigne oreille
En cette âpre saison
Reçoi nostre oraison:
Ou bien sus les Tartares,
Turcs, Scytes, & Barbares
Qui n'ont la cognoissance
Du bruit de ta puissance,
O Seigneur hardiment
Épan ce chatiment,
Et ton peuple console
Qui croit en ta parolle,
Ou fai encor renaistre
Les ans du premier estre,
L'age d'or precieus,
Où le peuple ocieus
Vivoit aus bois sans peine
De glan cheut & de feine.

Father, we understand
How far our daily faults
Contrary to your laws
Are horrible and grave:
And since we see the sins
With which our souls are stained
We know this present harm
Is less than we have earned.
But we know this as well.
Your mercy will befall
As many times as we
Go down upon our knees,
And raising up our faces,
Beseech you for your grace.
God, watch out over us
And let a gentle ear
During this harsh season
Be witness to our prayer;
Or cast this punishment
Oh Lord, with your hard hand,
On the Barbarian brood:
Scyths, Tartars, and the Turks,
Who have not understood
The grandeur of your works.
Bring your people comfort,
For we believe your word;
Or bring to birth again
The years of our first being,
The age of precious gold,
When gentle people could
Live simply in the woods;
Acorns, beech nuts their food.

6.

Qui voudra voyr comme un Dieu me surmonte,
     Comme il m'assault, comme il se fait vainqueur,
     Comme il r'enflamme, & r'englace mon cuœur,
     Comme il reçoit un honneur de ma honte,

Qui voudra voir une jeunesse prompte
     A suyvre en vain l'object de son malheur,
     Me vienne voir : il voirra ma douleur,
     Et la rigueur de l'Archer qui me donte.

Il cognoistra combien la raison peult
     Contre son arc, quand une foys il veult
     Que nostre cuœur son esclave demeure:

Et si voirra que je suis trop heureux,
     D'avoir au flanc l'aiguillon amoureux,
     Plein du venin dont il fault que je meure.

You want to see the effect of the God's
Riding me; his attack; his self-made
Vanquishing; how he kindles and chills my heart,
Takes honor from my shame:

To see quick youthfulness
Follow his sadness' object pointlessly?
Come look at me. You will see the wound
And the strength of the bowman.

You will learn the fragility of the mind's defense
Against his bow; for he has willed
Our hearts to last in slavery to him.

And you will notice that I am over happy
To have this arrow in my side,
Poisoned with love; and that it will kill me.

7.

Je veulx darder par l'univers ma peine,
   Plus tost qu'un trait ne volle au descocher:
   Je veulx de miel mes oreilles boucher
   Pour n'ouir plus la voix de ma Sereine.

Je veulx muer mes deux yeulx en fontaine,
   Mon cuœur en feu, ma teste en un rocher,
   Mes piedz en tronc, pour jamais n'aprocher
   De sa beaulté si fierement humaine.

Je veulx changer mes pensers en oyseaux,
   Mes doux souspirs en zephyres nouveaux,
   Qui par le monde evanteront ma pleinte.

Et veulx encor de ma palle couleur,
   Dessus le Loyr enfanter une fleur,
   Qui de mon nom & de mon mal soit peinte.

I want to flash my pain through the universe
With more speed than an arrow makes its mark.
I want to block my ears with honey;
Not listen to the Siren's voice any more.

I want to shift my eyes and make them springs,
Make my heart fire, make my head stone,
My feet a rooted tree, so I may not come near
Her proudly human beauty.

I want to shift my thinking into birds,
My sighing into new soft winds
To hoist my sorrow across the world.

I want to father a flower on the Loir,
Of my pale color, and let it be stained after
With my own name, and with my sadness.

8.

Je vouldroy bien richement jaunissant
En pluye d'or goute à goute descendre
Dans le beau sein de ma belle Cassandre,
Lors qu'en ses yeulx le somne va glissant.

Je vouldroy bien en toreau blanchissant
Me transformer pour finement la prendre,
Quand elle va par l'herbe la plus tendre
Seule à l'escart mille fleurs ravissant.

Je vouldroy bien afin d'aiser ma peine
Estre un Narcisse, & elle une fontaine
Pour m'y plonger une nuict à sejour:

Et vouldroy bien que ceste nuict encore
Durast tousjours sans que jamais l'Aurore
D'un front nouveau nous r'allumast le jour.

I would like to become ripe yellow rain
And fall, one golden drop after another
Into Cassandra's lovely lap
While sleep gathered and glided in her eyes.

I would like to become the good white bull
To take her cannily
When she came walking through the softest grass
Alone in her own quarter, gathering flowers.

And finally, to give my pain some easing
I would be a narcissus; she a spring
That I could plunge into and rest the night through.

And that one night would last forever.
There would never be dawn again
To make day flame before our faces.

9.

Plus tost le bal de tant d'astres divers
    Sera lassé, plus tost la terre & l'onde,
    Et du grand Tout l'ame en tout vagabonde
    Animera les abysmes ouverts:

Plus tost les cieulx des mers seront couverts,
    Plus tost sans forme ira confus le monde:
    Que je soys serf d'une maistresse blonde,
    Ou que j'adore une femme aux yeulx verds.

Car cest œil brun qui vint premier esteindre
    Le jour des miens, les sceut si bien attaindre,
    Qu'autre œil jamais n'en sera le vainqueur.

Et quant la mort m'aura la vie ostée,
    Encor là bas je veulx aymer l'Idée
    De ces beaulx yeulx que j'ay fichez au cuœur.

The dance of all the various stars will weary
And unravel; earth and sea,
The soul of the great All that flows through all
Will infuse life into the black holes:

The skies be covered up in oceans,
The world dissolve into its formless mass;
Before I be a slave to a blonde woman
Or fall in love with green-eyed lady.

It was a brown eye that first put out
Daylight from mine; knew so well how to reach me
No other eye could later conquer mine.

When death has lifted the life out of me
I would still will to love the kept image
Of the fine eyes I have fixed in my heart.

10.

Avant qu'Amour, du Chaos otieux
    Ouvrist le sein, qui couvoit la lumiere,
    Avec la terre, avec l'onde premiere,
    Sans art, sans forme, estoyent brouillez les cieulx.

Ainsi mon tout erroit seditieux
    Dans le giron de ma lourde matiere,
    Sans art, sans forme, & sans figure entiere,
    Alors qu'Amour le perça de ses yeulx.

Il arondit de mes affections
    Les petitz corps en leurs perfections,
    Il anima mes pensers de sa flamme.

Il me donna la vie, & le pouvoyr,
    Et de son branle il fit d'ordre mouvoyr
    Les pas suyviz du globe de mon ame.

Before Love opened the ribs of inert Chaos,
Who brooded light, the earth and the first sea
Shuffled about the heavens without form or art.

And so my all wandered seditiously
Within the husk of heavy corporal matter
Without form or art: without integral shape:
Until love broke through, piercing with his eyes.

Love ranked the atoms, the small perfect bodies
Of my affections, in a ring. His flame
Infused his spirit into my thinking.

Love gave life to me. It gave me power
And called the order of this perfect dance
Where all steps skirt the sphere my spirit is.

11.

Je veus brusler pour m'en voler aux cieux,
  Tout l'imparfait de ceste escorce humain
  M'eternisant, comme le filz d'Alcméne,
  Qui tout en feu s'assit entre les Dieux.

Ja mon esprit chatouillé de son mieux,
  Dedans ma chair, rebelle se promeine,
  Et ja le bois de sa victime ameine
  Pour s'enflammer aux rayons de tes yeulx.

O sainct brazier, ô feu chastement beau,
  Las, brusle moy d'un si chaste flambeau
  Qu'abandonant ma despouille cognue,

Nét, libre, & nud, je vole d'un plein sault,
  Oultre le ciel, pour adorer là hault
  L'aultre beaulté dont la tienne est venue.

I want to burn, and fly to heaven that way.
Burning will clarify the human wood,
Make me eternal, like Alcmene's son
Who all on fire sits with the gods around him.

My spirit is made urgent by its need
Within my body; tugs like a rebel at it;
Already drags the cut wood of its victim
To bring it to the flaming of your eyes.

Holy blaze, fire purely beautiful,
Burn me at last in such chaste flame
That I abandon my hacked flesh

Clear, free, and naked; and in a single bound
Fly beyond sky. And there I will adore
The other loveliness, from which yours comes.

12. FOLASTRIE

Jaquet ayme autant sa Robine
  Qu'une pucelle sa poupine,
  Robine ayme autant son Jaquet
  Qu'un amoureux fait son bouquet.
O amourettes doucelettes,
O doucelettes amourettes,
O couple d'amis bien heureux,
Ensemble aimez & amoureux.
O Robine bien fortunée
De s'estre au bon Jaquet donnée,
O bon Jaquet bien fortuné
De s'estre à Robine donné.
Que ny les cottes violettes,
Les ribans, ny les ceinturettes,
Les brasseletz, les chaperons,
Les devanteaux, les mancherons
N'ont eu la puissance d'epoindre
Pour macreaux ensemble les joindre.

Mais les rivages babillars,
  L'oisiveté des prez mignars,
  Les fonteines argentelettes,
  Qui attrainent leurs ondelettes
  Par un petit trac mousselet
  Du creux d'un antre verdelet,
  Les grans forestz renouvelées,
  Le solitaire des valées
  Closes d'éfroy tout alentour,
  Furent cause de telle amour.

En la saison que l'hyver dure,
  Tous deux, pour tromper la froidure,
  Au pié d'un chene mimangé,
  De main tramblante ont arrangé

Jacky loved his little Robin
Like a little girl her dolly.
Robin loved her little Jacky
Like a lover makes his nosegay.
Delicately loving lovers!
Lovers' love is delicate!
Heaven bless the happy pair
That loving love, and loved, are loving.

Oh Robin, blessed with happy luck
To be to Jacky happy given:
Oh happy Jacky blessed with luck
To be to his sweet Robin given.

It was not purple petticoats,
Nor ribbons, garters, bracelets, nor
Hats, aprons, lacy ornaments,
That had sufficient goading strength
To pimp them to exchange of coupling.

But babbling brooks and lazing fields;
The bubbling silver of the springs
That fingered all their little rills
Through mossy little hidden tracks
Into the ferny dark of caves;
The great re-greening forest trees;
The lonesome valley clenched with fright:
Were causes of such loving.

Harsh winter was the season. They
Together had to fight the cold.
At foot of a half rotted oak
With shivering fingers they arranged
Some stems of hemp, and some dried ferns,

Des chenevotes, des fougeres,
Des fueilles de Tramble legeres,
Des buchettes, & des brochars,
Et souflant le feu des deux pars
Chaufoient à fesses acropies
Le cler degout de leurs roupies.

Apres qu'ilz furent un petit
    Desangourdis, un apetit
    Se vint ruer dans la poitrine
    Et de Jaquet, & de Robine.

Robine tira de son sein
    Un gros quignon buret de pain,
    Qu'elle avoit fait de pure aveine
    Pour tout le long de la sepmaine:
    Et le trempant au just des aux,
    Et dans le brouet des poureaux,
    De l'autre costé reculée
    Mangeoit apart son éculée.

D'autre costé, Jaquet, espris
    D'une faim merveilleuse, a pris
    Du ventre de sa panetiere
    Une galette toute entiere,
    Cuitte sur les charbons du four,
    Et blanche de sel tout autour,
    Que Guillemine sa marraine
    Luy avoit donné pour estraine.
    Comme il repaissoit, il a veu,
    Guignant par le travers du feu,
    De sa Robine recourssée
    La grosse motte retroussée,
    Et son petit cas barbelu
    D'un or jaunement crespelu,
    Dont le fond sembloit une rose
    Non encor' à demy déclose.

Robine aussi, d'une autre part,
    De Jaquet guignoit le tribart,
    Qui luy pendoit entre les jambes,
    Plus rouge que les rouges flambes
    Qu'elle atisoit songneusement.

Handfulls of shaking aspen leaves,
Kindling and some hacked branches too,
And blew the fire from both sides.
Hunkering down upon their buttocks
They warmed the clear melt from their clothes.

After they were a little bit
Unnumbed, one found an appetite
Occurred at some point in the breasts
Of Jacky and his little Robin.

So Robin took out of her smock
A dark large hunk of whole-meal bread
Which she had made of simple oats,
One bread to last her the whole week:
She dipped it in the juice of garlic,
And in a boiled leeky broth,
And ate it, crouching in her place.

On the other side, young Jacky, smitten
With marvelous hunger, reached and found
Inside the pouch that held his bread
A good whole cake his godmother
Had cooked him on the charcoal stove
And coated all around with salt
And given as his New Year's present.

Now while he filled himself he saw
Peeping out from across the fire
Robin's grand and puckered hillock
And its little bearded case
Made of crisp gold curls, and yellow,
In whose midst there seemed a rose
Resting, and that not halfway closed.

Robin also from her side
Glimpsed her little Jacky's hobble
That hung down between his legs,
Redder than the reddest flames
She stirred up so carefully.
After she had watched enough
To see the scowl and heft of it
She did not think it not worth while;
Lifted a little bit her face
And made this motion to her Jacky.

Apres avoir veu longuement
Ce membre gros & renfrongné,
Robine ne l'a dedaigné,
Mais en levant un peu la teste
A Jaquet fist ceste requeste:

Jaquet (dit el'), que j'ayme mieux
Ny que mon cœur, ny que mes yeux,
Si tu n'aymes mieux ta galette
Que ta mignarde Robinette,
Je te pry, Jaquet, jauche moy,
Et metz le grand pau que je voy
Dedans le rond de ma fossette.

Helas (dit Jaquet) ma doucette,
Si plus cher ne t'est ton grignon
Que moy Jaquinot ton mignon,
Aproche toy, mignardelette,
Doucelette, paillardelette,
Mon pain, ma faim, mon apetit,
Pour mieux te chouser un petit.

A peine eut dit, qu'elle s'aproche,
Et le bon Jaquet qui l'embroche
Fist trepigner tous les Sylvains
Du dru maniment de ses reins.
Les boucs barbus qui l'agueterent,
Paillars, sur les chevres monterent,
Et ce Jaquet contr' aguignant
Alloient à l'envy trepignant.

O bien heureuses amourettes,
O amourettes doucelettes,
O couple d'amans bien heureux,
Ensemble aymez, & amoureux.
O Robine bien fortunée
De s'estre au bon Jaquet donnée,
O bon Jaquet bien fortuné
De s'estre à Robine donné,
O doucelettes amourettes,
O amourettes doucelettes.

Jacky, she said, you know I love you
More than my heart and both my eyes.
Unless you must prefer your cake
To your sweet darling Robin, please
Come cover me, I beg you, Jacky,
And dunk the dibble that I see
Into the round dip of my furrow.

Aha! said Jack; my little sweet;
If dearer to you is not your stew
Than me, your little lover Jack,
Come nearer little darling, sweet,
My charming little dirty darling,
My bread, my hunger, appetite,
So we may share a little better.

He'd hardly said it when she came
And her good Jacky skewered her,
And all the sylvan gods applaud
The heavy handling of his loins.
The bearded bucks who witnessed them
Wantonly mounted on their does.
As Jacky prodded steady on
They leaped in sympathetic dance.

Oh lovers greatly fortunate!
Delicately loving lovers!
Heaven bless the happy pair
That loving love, and loved, are loving!
Oh Robin, blessed with happy luck
To be to Jacky happy given;
Oh happy Jacky, blessed with luck,
To be to his sweet Robin given!
Oh, delicately loving lovers!

Lovers' love is delicate.

13. ODE A CASSANDRE

Mignonne, allon voir si la rose
    Qui ce matin avoit declose
    Sa robe de pourpre au soleil,
    A point perdu, cette vesprée,
    Les plis de sa robe pourprée,
    Et son teint au vostre pareil.

Las, voiés comme en peu d'espace,
    Mignonne, elle a dessus la place
    Las, las, ses beautés laissé choir!
    O vraiment maratre Nature,
    Puis qu'une telle fleur ne dure
    Que du matin jusques au soir.

Donc, si vous me croiés, mignonne:
    Tandis que vôtre âge fleuronne
    En sa plus verte nouveauté,
    Cueillés, cueillés vôtre jeunesse
    Comme à cette fleur, la vieillesse
    Fera ternir vôtre beauté.

Darling, we'll go together, see if this morning's
New opened rose—it opened crimson to the sun—
Has lost its crimson pleatings now that it is evening;
See if its color has become less than yours is.

Darling, we find how short a stretch of time
Its beauty lasts. Loveliness is let fall.
This nature's mothering is bitter: such a flower
Survives only from morning into the first evening.

Old age will shrivel you, as it does this flower.
Therefore, if you would put some trust in me, darling,
You must take youngness: you must gather it in
While you are green, and while your newness flowers.

14. ÉPITRE
A AMBROISE DE LA PORTE PARISIEN.

Encependant que le pesteux Automne
    Tes citoiens l'un sur l'autre moissonne,
    Et que Caron a les bras tout lassés
    D'avoir deja tant de Manes passés,
    Ici, fuiant ta vile perilleuse
    Je suis venu pres de Marne l'ileuse,
    Non guere loin de la part, où ses eaus
    D'un bras fourchu pressent les murs de Meaus:
    Meaus, dont Bacus songneus a pris la garde,
    Et d'un bon œil ses colines regarde
    Riches de vin qui n'est point surmonté
    Du vin d'Aï en friande bonté.
    Non seulement Bacus les favorise,
    Mais sa Compagne, & le pasteur d'Anfrise,
    L'une y faisant les épis blondoïer,
    L'autre à foison les herbes verdoier.

Dés le matin que l'Aube safranée
    A du beau jour la clarté ramenée,
    Et dés midi jusque aus raions couchans
    Tout égaré je me pers dans les chams,
    A humer l'air, à voir les belles prées,
    A contempler les colines pamprées,
    A voir de loing la charge des pommiers
    Présque rompus de leurs fruis Autonniers,
    A repousser sur l'herbe verdelette
    De tour de bras l'éteuf d'une palette,
    A voir couler sur Marne les bateaus,
    A me cacher dans le jonc des îleaus:
    Ore je sui quelque lievre à la trace,
    Or' la perdris je couvre à la tirace,
    Or' d'une ligne apâtant l'ameçon
    Loin haut de l'eau j'enleve le poisson,

for Bill and Catherine McGurn

Now Autumn's plagues
Crop down your fellow citizens crosswise,
And Charon's arms give out
With ferrying souls.
I've come to escape your perilous city,
To this Marne, well islanded.
Not far from here the forked arm's water
Bathes the foundation of the town of Meaux—
A town that careful Bacchus guards:
Whose good eye blessed its hills
With precious wine. Even the wine of Ay
Cannot surpass its delicacy.
Not only Bacchus blesses it,
But his companion, Ceres, blondes
Her tall wheat there; and shepherd
Apollo makes abundant forage green.

Dawn saffrons the sky at morning
And brings a day's clear air.
And I am in it still at noon; and still
When the light rests
I'm wandering, completely taken, through plowed
Fields, drinking the air, watching these meadows,
Hills terraced in vineyards.
From far away the heavy apple trees
Seem almost broken with their autumn burden.

(I bounce my tennis ball
With arm and racket, against green grass.)

Hiding along an island's reedy banks
I watch boats flowing on the Marne.
I follow rabbit tracks,
Or take a partridge in my net;

Or' dans les trous d'une île tortuese
Je va charchant l'écrevice cancreuse,
Or' je me baigne, ou couché sur les bors
Sans y penser à l'envers je m'endors:
Puis reveillé ma guitterre je touche,
Et m'adossant contre une vieille souche,
Je di les vers que Tityre chantoit
Quand pres d'Auguste encores il n'estoit,
Et qu'il pleuroit au mantouan rivage,
Deja barbu, son desert heritage.
Ainsi jadis Alexandre le blond,
Le beau Paris apuié sur un tronc
Harpoit, alors qu'il vit parmi les nues
Venir à lui les trois Déesses nues:
Devant les trois Mercure le premier
Partissoit l'air de son pié talonnier,
Aiant es mains la pomme d'or saisie,
Le commun mal d'Europe, & de l'Asie.
Mais d'autant plus que poete j'aime mieus
Le bon Bacus que tous les autres Dieus,
Sur tous plaisirs la vandange m'agrée,
A voir tomber cette manne pourprée
Qu'à piés dechaus un gacheur fait couler
Dedans la cuve à force de fouler.

Sur les coustaus marche d'ordre une troupe,
L'un les raisins d'une serpette couppe,
L'autre les porte en sa hote au pressoüer,
L'un tout au tour du pivot fait roüer
La viz qui geint, l'autre le marc asserre
En un monceau, & d'ais pressés le serre,
L'un met à l'anche un panier ataché,
L'autre reçoit le pepin ecaché,
L'un tient le mui, l'autre le vin entonne,
Un bruit se fait, le pressoüer en resonne.

Vela, la porte, en quels plaisirs je suis
Or' que ta vile epovanté je fuis,
Or' que l'Autonne épenche son usure,
Et que la Livre à juste pois mesure
La nuit egale, avec les jours egaus,
Et que les jours ne sont ne frois ne chaus.

With hook and line, haul fish out of the water,
Or go exploring for the cancrous crayfish
In the holes of a twisted island.
Sometimes I swim, or without intending to
I fall asleep upside down on the bank.

Waking again, I play my guitar,
Leaning against some ancient stump.
I speak the lines Virgil had Tityrus sing
Weeping beside the waters of Mantua,
Lamenting his abandoned patrimony,
Far from Augustus: his beard beginning already.
So light-haired Alexander
(Homer's Paris), propped against tree trunk,
Harped till he saw among the clouds
Three naked goddesses approaching,
Mercury leading, parting the air with his winged foot,
His hand holding the stolen golden apple,
Europe's and Asia's common loss.

Being a poet, I love Bacchus more than all other gods.
The grape harvest has pleased me above everything.
This purple manna falls.
The barefoot trampler thrusts
The beaten gush of juice into the vat.

Battalions march in order upon the hillsides.
One cuts the grapes with pruning knives;
Another humps them to the presses in a basket.
One turns the wheel around its whining screw,
Another piles the squeezed marc, presses it with a plank;
One holds a straining-basket to the spigot,
Another takes the crushed seeds;
One holds the hogshead, another empties wine in.
And the whole press resounds with the brilliant noise of it.

And so, la Porte, I am in such pleasure now,
Even though terror drove me from your city,
Now that Autumn pours out her fruits with interest,
And Libra measures with fair weights,
Balances night and day with equal hours;
Makes day neither hot nor cold.

Quelque plaisir toutesfois qui me tienne,
Faire ne puis qu'il ne me resouvienne
De ton Paris, & que tousjours ecrit
Ce grand Paris ne soit en mon esprit.
Et te promets que si tôt que la bise
Hors de son bois aura la fueille mise,
Faisant des prés la verte robe choir,
Que d'un pié pront je courrai pour revoir
Mes compagnons, & mes livres, que j'aime
Beaucoup plus qu'eus, que toi, ne que moimême.

Such pleasure holds me;
But it will not dislodge
My memory of your Paris,
Nor keep it from being written always in my mind.

I promise as soon as the north wind
Has swept forests clear of leaves,
And made the fields' green dresses fall,
I'll be back quickly, and revisit
My friends, my books—
Which I love more than these fields, than you;
More than myself.

15. EPITAFE DE FRANÇOIS RABELAIS.

Si d'un mort qui pourri repose
    Nature engendre quelque chose,
    Et si la generation
    Se fait de la corruption,
    Une vigne prendra naissance
    De l'estomac et de la pance
    Du bon Rabelais, qui boivoit
    Tousjours ce pendant qu'il vivoit.

La fosse de sa grande gueule
    Eust plus beu de vin toute seule
    (L'epuisant du nez en deus cous)
    Qu'un porc ne hume de lait dous,
    Qu'Iris de fleuves, ne qu'encore
    De vagues le rivage more.

Jamais le Soleil ne l'a veu,
    Tant fût-il matin, qu'il n'eust beu,
    Et jamais au soir la nuit noire,
    Tant fut tard, ne l'a veu sans boire.
    Car, alteré, sans nul sejour
    Le gallant boivoit nuit & jour.

Mais quand l'ardante Canicule
    Ramenoit la saison qui brule,
    Demi-nus se troussoit les bras,
    Et se couchoit tout plat à bas
    Sur la jonchée, entre les taces:
    Et parmi des escuelles grasses
    Sans nulle honte se touillant,
    Alloit dans le vin barbouillant
    Comme une grenouille en sa fange:

From the disintegrating resting dead
If Nature engender anything,
Corruption foster generation—
From the pot belly and staunch gut
Of good Rabelais, grape vine will grow.
For he drank all the time he lived.

The ditch of his grand gawp drank in
Working alone (although his nose
Pumped in some extra), much more wine
Than a pig sucks in of sweet milk,
Than rainbows suck water from streams:
More than the dirt the rivers gnaw.

Black night and sunshine did not find
A morning or an evening when
Early or late, he was not drinking.
His thirsty throat worked faithfully.
The gallant man took no vacation.

And when the glowing little dog
Brought out the summer sun to burn,
Half naked, with his sleeves rolled up,
We'd find him couched among the rushes,
Proudly surrounded by his cups
And empty hefty porringers.
He soaked and sullied shamelessly;
Would daub and scribble in his wine
As happy as a frog in muck.
And then he sang his drunken songs
About good Bacchus, his old friend,
And how he beat the Thebans down;
And how his Dad took on his Ma
Too hot, too hot; he burned her live
Instead of doing that thing with her.

Puis ivre chantoit la louange
De son ami le bon Bacus,
Comme sous lui furent vaincus
Les Thebains, & comme sa mere
Trop chaudement receut son pere,
Qui en lieu de faire cela,
Las! toute vive la brula.

Il chantoit la grande massüe,
Et la jument de Gargantüe,
Son fils Panurge, & les païs
Des Papimanes ébaïs:
Et chantoit les Iles Hieres
Et frere Jan des autonnieres,
Et d'Episteme les combas:
Mais la mort qui ne boivoit pas
Tira le beuveur de ce monde,
Et ores le fait boire en l'onde
Qui fuit trouble dans le giron
Du large fleuve d'Acheron.

Or toi quiconques sois qui passes
Sur sa fosse repen des taces,
Repen du bril, & des flacons,
Des cervelas, & des jambons,
Car si encor dessous la lame
Quelque sentiment a son ame,
Il les aime mieus que des Lis,
Tant soient ils fraichement cueillis.

He sang Gargantua's great club,
He sang his mare, his giant son,
The land of dumbfound Papimanes.
He sang the Isles of yesterdays
And Friar John of Antoumeures;
The battles of Epistemon.

But death, who is himself no drunk,
Gathered the drinker from the world;
Set him to drinking in the waves
That flow cloudily in the lap
Of the deep river Acheron.

Well, when you pass his grave, you should
Leave cups and flasks of sparkling wine,
Salamis, hams: his spirit may
Retain some feeling under this
Stone; and he'd love those presents more
Than lilies, even freshly killed.

16. EPITAFE DE JAQUES MERNABLE,
JOUEUR DE FARCES.

Tandis que tu vivois, Mernable,
  Tu n'avois ni maison, ne table,
  Et jamais, pauvre, tu n'as veu
  En ta maison le pot au feu.
  Ores la mort t'est proufitable,
  Car tu n'as plus besoing de table,
  Ni de pot, & si desormais
  Tu as maison pour tout jamais.

Mernable, all the time you lived
In poverty, you had no table
Nor any home; you never saw
The stewpot bubbling in your house.

And so your death is profitable.
You will no longer want the pot;
Nor do you have much need for tables:
But you have an eternal house.

17.

Cache pour cette nuit ta corne, bonne Lune,
   Ainsi Endemion soit toujours ton ami
   Et sans se reveiller en ton sein endormi:
   Ainsi nul Enchanteur jamais ne t'importune.

Le jour m'est odieus, la nuit m'est oportune,
   Je crains de jour l'aguet d'un voisin ennemi,
   De nuit plus courageus je traverse parmi
   Le camp des espions, defendu de la brune.

Tu sçais, Lune, que peut l'amoureuse poison,
   Le Dieu Pan, pour le pris d'une blanche toison
   Peut bien fléchir ton cœur, & vous Astres insignes

Favorisés au feu qui me tient alumé:
   Car s'il vous en souvient, la pluspart de vous, Signes,
   Ne se voit luire au ciel que pour avoir aimé.

This night should hide the good moon's horns.
Horns, breasts. Endymion might lay his head in darkness
There, and be your lover still, despite all magic.

Daylight is awful to me. I fear the watch of the close enemy.
Night lets my sly wanderings take me, wreathed in dusk,
Among the camps of spies, bravely.

Your heart was bent and pierced. You know
Love's poisonous subterfuge, the trading and pricing:
The Goat God took you in on a white sheep skin.

The stars spin. They and I are locked in the same fire.
It is love that placed and holds us in deep space.

18.

Cesse tes pleurs, mon livre, il n'est pas ordonné
    Du destin, que moi vif tu reçoives ta gloire:
    Avant que passé j'aye outre la rive noire,
    L'honneur que l'on te doit ne te sera donné.

Apres mille ans je voi que quelcun étonné
    En mes vers de bien loin viendra de mon Loir boire,
    Et voiant mon païs à peine voudra croire
    Que d'un si petit champ tel poëte soit né.

Pren, mon livre, pren cœur, la vertu precieuse
    » De l'homme quand il vit est toujours odieuse:
    » Mais apres qu'il est mort chacun le pense un Dieu.

» La rancueur nuit toujours à ceus qui sont en vie,
    » Sur les vertus d'un mort elle n'a plus de lieu,
    » Et la posterité rend l'honneur sans envie.

My words are weeping. That must stop.
Destiny has not ordered my work known or respected
During my lifetime. No honor comes
To a man's work, before he sinks past the black river.

After a thousand years, my poems will surprise
Someone who comes that way into my country,
Drinks magic water in my Loir, looks
Over my land: astonished, discovers the tiny field

Ronsard bragged he was born in. Heart, book:
A living man is hated for his precious skill
Until his death has made a god of him in people's thinking.

I will be dead, and who can envy me then?
I'll have my honor without rancor.

19. LA GRENOUILLE
A REMY BELLEAU DU PERCHE.

Nous t'estimons une Déesse,
    Chere Grenouille, qui sans cesse
    Au fonds des ruisselets herbeus
    Te desalteres quand tu veus:
    Et jamais la soif vehemente
    Qui l'Esté les gorges tourmente
    Du pauvre peuple & des grans Rois
    Ne te tourmente, car tu bois
    (Hé Dieu que je porte d'envie
    Aus felicités de ta vie)
    A gorge ouverte, sous les eaus
    Comme la Roine des Ruisseaus.

Quand tu es sur la rive herbüe
    Aus raix du soleil estendüe
    Que tu es aise ! Si un beuf
    Passe par là mourant de seuf,
    Tu enfles contre la grand beste
    Si fort les venes de la teste,
    Et coaçes d'un si haut bruit,
    Que de crainte le beuf s'enfuit,
    Toi demeurant sus l'herbe espesse
    Des rives la seule maistresse.

En ton royaume le serpent
    Te combat, mais il se repent
    Tout sus l'heure de t'avoir prise,
    Car tu luy tiens la teste mise
    Si long tans au fond du ruisseau,
    Que tu l'estouffes dessous l'eau.

for Janet and Lowry Burgess

We think you are a goddess, frog
Darling, because you quench your thirst
At bottom in the grassy streams;
And never does the dreadful drought
Of Summer, that torments the throats
Of common people and great kings
Torment you, frog, because you drink
(Oh, God, how much I envy you
Your life of such felicity)
With open throat, beneath the waves,
As if you were the queen of streams.

When you are on the grassy bank
Stretched out at full length in the sun,
How lazy your life! If a cow
Comes by your spot, half dead from thirst,
You puff the veins up in your head
Against the great beast, and you croak
With such a greek and hearty noise
That the cow tears away in fright
While you stay under matted grass,
Sole mistress of the river banks.

Into your kingdom comes the snake
To fight against you; but he soon
Repents his catching you, because
You hold his head for him so long
Down at the bottom of the stream
You drown him underneath the waves.

En vain le Heron t'est contraire,
   T'espiant du bord solitaire
   De quelque estang, car il ne peut
   Te digerer lors qu'il le veut,
   Et vive est contraint de te rendre
   Pour fuir, quand on le vient prendre.

Cela, Grenoille, que tu vois
   Et par les chams, & par les bois
   Est pour toy, & ce que les prées,
   Ce que tiennent les eaus sacrées
   De bon, en leur profond recoy,
   N'est fait, Grenoille, que pour toy.

Le laboureur à ta venüe
   Joyeus de ton chant te salüe
   Comme profette du printans:
   Ores tu predis le beau tans
   Ore la pluye, ore l'orage:
   Jamais ton groin ne fait doumage
   A fleur, à plante, ni à fruit,
   N'a rien que la terre ait produit:
   Tu vaus trop plus en medecine
   Qu'herbe, qu'onguent, ni que racine:
   Et ton profitable fiel
   Est au malade un don du ciel:
   Tu vaus contre le mal d'Hercule,
   Ton gesier les venins recule
   De ceulx qu'empoisonner on veut:
   Ta langue charmeresse peut
   Faire conter à la pucelle
   Les propos que veut sçavoir d'elle
   Le jeune amant qui la poursuit,
   La lui pendant au col de nuit.

Bref, que dirai-je plus? ta vie
   N'est comme la nostre asservie
   A la longueur du tans malin,
   Car bien tost, bien tost tu prends fin:
   Et nous trainons nos destinées
   Quelquesfois quatre vins années,
   Et cent années quelquesfois,
   Et tu ne dures que six mois

The heron is your opposite
In vain (he finds you all alone
Upon a pond's bank); for he can't
Digest you, even though he wishes,
And is constrained to give you up
Alive, to flee from his own captor.

My dear frog, all things that you see
Throughout the fields and woods are yours;
Whatever meadows have in store,
Whatever sacred waters hold
Of value down inside their deeps
Is only made, dear frog, for you.

The plowman, when he hears you sing,
Salutes you. You have made him glad.
You are the prophet of the Spring.
You tell of fair weather to come,
Or warn of approaching storm or rain.
Your ugly mug can do no harm
To fruit, to flower, nor to plant;
To nothing, in fact, the earth produces.
And you do more for medicine
Than herbs, or roots, or precious oils.

The profitable bile you have
Is heaven's gift to invalids,
And works to heal epilepsy.
Your gizzard makes unvenomous
The poisons used to poison people.
Your tongue has got the magic gift
To make a girl tell what her lover
Wishes her to, as long as he
Hangs it at nighttime on her neck.

There's more that I can say. Your life
Is not made subject, as is ours,
To long duration of hard times:
Because you reach your finish soon!
We must drag out our destinies
Sometimes as much as eighty years,
Even a hundred years sometimes,

Franche du tans, & de la peine
A laquelle la gent humaine
Est endétée, des le jour
Qu'elle entre en ce commun sejour.

*   *   *

Or si quelcun doit recevoir
    Quelque salaire pour avoir
    D'un autre chanté la louange,
    Octroye moy pour contre échange
    De mes vers, un present nouveau
    Aus premiers mois du renouveau:
    C'est que ta vois un petit rude
    N'aproche jamais de l'estude,
    Ni du lit, de mon cher Belleau.

Ainsi, Grenouille, ainsi dans l'eau
    Le Heron bécu ne te gripe,
    Et le brochet dedans sa tripe
    Jamais ne te puisse enfoüir,
    Et tousjours puisses tu fuyr
    La piece rouge hameçonnée,
    Et jamais le sale hymenée
    Du crapaut, de venin couvert,
    Ne puisse souiller ton dôs vert.

While you don't last more than six months:
Time's Independent! free from the pain
The human race is subject to
Since we began as tenants here.

Now, if somebody should receive
A salary for having sung
The praises of some other one,
Then grant me as the recompense
You give me for this poem, this
New gift, to last through the spring months:
Prevent your somewhat grating voice
From coming near the bed or study
Of my good friend Rémy Belleau.

And so, good frog, so, in your wave,
May the beaked heron never get you;
And let the pike not have his chance
To pleat your body in his gut.
And may you manage to escape
The red cloth bait of froggers' hooks.
And may the filthy wedding slime
Of toadies, thick and poisonous,
Not fall to sully your green back.

20. ODE
A JACQUES DE RUBAMPRÉ.

Puis que tost je doi reposer
　　Outre l'infernale riviere,
　　É que me sert de composer
　　Autant de vers qu'a fait Homere?

Les vers ne me sauveront pas,
　　Qu'ombre poudreuse je ne sente
　　Combien Rhadamante a là bas
　　La main & la bouche pesante.

Je pose la cas que mes vers,
　　De mon labeur en contre-change,
　　Dix ou vint ans par l'univers
　　M'aportent un peu de louange:

Que faut-il pour la consumer,
　　Et pour mon livre oter de terre,
　　Qu'un feu qui le vienne alumer,
　　Ou qu'un esclandre de la guerre?

Suis-je meilleur qu'Anacreon,
　　Que Stesichore, ou Simonide,
　　Ou qu'Antimache, ou que Bion,
　　Que Philete, ou que Bachylide?

Toutesfois bien qu'ils fussent Grés
　　Que leur servit leur beau langage?
　　De rien, puisque les ans d'apres
　　Ont du tout perdu leur ouvrage.

Donque moi qui suis né François,
　　Composeur de rimes barbares,
　　Hé doi-je esperer que ma voix
　　Surmonte les siecles avares?

for Christopher

Since I must soon be sleeping
Beyond the infernal river
What use is it to write
As many lines as Homer?

Poetry will not save me
From the dust's shadow, heavy
Already in the fingers
And mouth of Rhadamanthus.

Suppose my labor's poems
May find some recognition
For ten or twenty years:
Praise is exchange for working?

My books, to be consumed
And raised like smoke to heaven:
Must they be burned in fire,
Or ride on battles' terrors?

Am I a better poet
Than Bion, Stesichorus,
Anacreon, Philetus,
Bachylides, Simonides,
Even Antimachus?

Although these men were Greeks,
What use was their fine language?
Useless: the work of all
Has perished in the meantime.

Non non, il vaut mieux, Rubampré,
    Son age en trafiques despendre,
    Ou davant un Senat Pourpré
    Pour de l'argent sa langue vendre,

Que de suivre l'ocieux train
    De cette pauvre Caliope,
    Qui toujours fait mourir de faim
    Les meilleurs chantres de sa trope.

How can a Frenchman born
Barbarian composer
Be hopeful that his voice
Will ride the greedy ages?

Much better, Rubampré,
To use my years in business,
Or spend my tongue for money
Before the purple Senate,

Than follow in the train of
Calliope's simple paupers:
For she kills off, by hunger,
Her company's best singers.

21. ODELETTE
A L'ARONDELLE

Tai toi, babillarde Arondelle,
    Par Dieu je plumerai ton aile
    Si je t'empongne, ou d'un couteau
    Je te couperai ta languette,
    Qui matin sans repos caquette
    Et m'estourdit tout le cerveau.

Je te preste ma cheminée
    Pour chanter toute la journée,
    De soir, de nuit, quand tu voudras:
    Mais au matin ne me reveille,
    Et ne m'oste quand je sommeille
    Ma Cassandre d'entre mes bras.

for Jacob

Shut up, you noisy swallow.
By God, I'll pull your wings off,
If I can catch you. Your tongue
I'll clip off with my penknife.
You cackle all the morning
And make my whole head giddy.

I offer you my chimney
To sing the whole day through on
As you like, night and evening.
Don't wake me in the morning
And snatch, while I am sleeping,
Cassandra from my pillow.

22. ODELETTE

La terre les eaux va boivant,
    L'arbre la boit par sa racine,
    La mer eparse boit le vent,
    Et le Soleil boit la marine.

Le Soleil est beu de la Lune:
    Tout boit, soit en haut ou en bas:
    Suivant cette reigle commune
    Pourquoi donc ne boiron nous pas?

The earth drinks water. Trees
Drink earth up through their roots.
The frothy waves drink wind
And the sun drinks the seas.

The sun is drunk by moon.
All drink, both high and low.
This is our common law.
Why aren't we drinking, then?

23. ODE
A SA MAITRESSE.

Plusieurs de leurs cors denués
    Se sont veuz en diverse terre
    Miraculeusement mués,
    L'un en serpent, & l'autre en pierre,

L'un en fleur, l'autre en arbrisseau,
    L'un en loup, l'autre en colombelle,
    L'un se vit changer en ruisseau,
    Et l'autre devint arondelle.

Mais je voudrois estre miroir,
    Afin que toujours tu me visses:
    Chemise je voudrois me voir,
    Afin que toujours tu me prisses.

Voulentiers eau je deviendrois
    Afin que ton cors je lavasse,
    Estre du parfum je voudrois
    Afin que je te parfumasse.

Je voudrois estre le riban
    Qui serre ta belle poitrine:
    Je voudrois estre le carquan
    Qui orne ta gorge ivoirine.

Je voudrois estre tout autour
    Le coural qui tes levres touche,
    Afin de baiser nuit & jour
    Tes belles levres & ta bouche.

Various of their freed bodies
Discovered themselves in strange countries
Marvelously changed
To snakes and stones,

Flowers, shrubs, a wolf,
Dove: one found himself a stream,
One was a swallow.

I'd be a mirror.
You would look into me always.
I could be your shirt.
You would wear me.

Delightfully, I would become
Water while I bathed your body;
Be the perfume of you,
Give you my scent.

I'd be the ribbon binding
Your lovely breasts; I'd be
The necklace marking your
Ivory throat.

I want to be the coral
That your lips are touching.
All night and day I would be kissing
Sweet lips and mouth.

24. ODE

Ma douce jouvance est passée,
   Ma premiere force est cassée,
   J'ai la dent noire, & le chef blanc,
   Mes nerfs sont dissous, & mes venes,
   Tant j'ai le cors froid, ne sont plenes
   Que d'une eau rousse, en lieu de sang.

Adieu ma Lyre, adieu fillettes,
   Jadis mes douces amourettes,
   Adieu, je sen venir ma fin,
   Nul passetans de ma jeunesse
   Ne m'acompagne en la vieillesse,
   Que le feu, le lit, & le vin.

J'ai la teste toute élourdie
   De trop d'ans, & de maladie,
   De tous costés le soin me mord:
   Et soit que j'aille ou que je tarde
   Toujours derriere moi regarde
   Si je verrai venir la mort,

Qui doit, ce me semble, à toute heure
   Me mener là bas où demeure
   Je ne sçai quel Pluton, qui tient
   Ouvert à tous venans un antre
   Où bien facilement on entre,
   Mais d'où jamais on ne revient.

Sweet youthfulness is past.
My early powers are bust;
Black-toothed and white of head
Nerves raveled, and my veins
Corpse cold, filled up with red
Water in place of blood.

My little girls, goodbye;
Old lovers; and my lyre.
I feel the end is near.
The pastimes of the boy
That fit the old man's need
Are fire and wine and bed.

Now heavy is my mind
With age and illnesses.
On every hand is stress.
Whether I stall or run,
I keep a watch behind
To see if death is come.

He will take me for sure
Below there where some kind
Of Pluto waits. His hand
Holds open the cave door
That lets all comers in.
We won't come back again.

25. HYMNE DES ASTRES.
A MELIN DE SAINCT GELAIS

Vers heroiques

C'est trop long temps, Mellin, demeuré sur la terre
    Dans l'humaine prison, qui l'Esprit nous enserre,
    Le tenant engourdy d'un sommeil ocieux
    Il faut le delïer, & l'envoyer aux cieux:
    Il me plaist en vivant de voir souz moy les nües,
    Et presser de mes pas les espaules chenües
    D'Atlas le porte-ciel, il me plaist de courir
    Jusques au Firmament, & les secretz ouvrir
    (S'il m'est ainsi permis) des Astres admirables,
    Et chanter leurs regardz de noz destins coupables:
    Pour t'en faire un present Mellin, enfant du Ciel,
    Mellin, qui pris ton nom de la douceur du meil
    Qu'au berceau tu mangeas, quand en lieu de nourrice
    L'Abeille te repeut de thin & de melisse.
    Aussi je ferois tort à mes vers, & à moy,
    Si je les consacrois à un autre qu'à toy,
    Qui sçais le cours du Ciel, & congnois les puissances
    Des Astres dont je parle, & de leurs influences.

Des le commencement (s'il faut le croire ainsi)
    Les Estoilles n'avoient noz destins en soucy,
    Et n'avoient point encor de tout ce Monde large,
    Comme ell' ont aujourd'huy, ny le soing ny la charge:
    Sans plus elles flamboyent pour un bel ornement,
    Eparses, sans vertu, par tout le Firmament.
    Quand le Soleil hurtoit des Indes les barrieres
    Sortant de l'Ocean, les Heures ses portieres
    Couroient un peu devant son lumineux flambeau
    R'amasser par le Ciel des Astres le troupeau,
    Qui demenoit la dance, & les contoient par nombre,
    Ainsi que les pasteurs, qui, le matin, souz l'ombre
    D'un chesne, vont contant leurs brebis & leurs bœufz,
    Ains que les mener paistre aux rivages herbeux.

for Leo Kelley

The world locks us into our human prison
Too long, Melin; keeps my soul dull in heavy sleep.
I must unlace her and let her float freely.
I would enjoy the look of the clouds under me,
Make footprints in the snow on Atlas's shoulders.
I would enjoy the long run to hard heaven's edge,
The firmament, where I would open the stars'
Admirable secrets, if that were allowed me,
And sing their guilty watch over our destinies,
And make a present of it for you. You are heaven's child,
Whose name comes from the gentleness of honey, taken
In the cradle, bee-made of thyme and melisse.
You know the sky's roads, and you know the power of stars,
And their influences. I consecrate this poem to you.

At the beginning, the stars cared nothing for our destiny,
Nor had they charge over the world's working, as they do today,
But hung burning simply, simple decoration,
Scattered and powerless, throughout the firmament.
When the sun broke the walls of the Indies, and leaped
Out of the ocean, the hours attended him.
They ran ahead of his flaming torch to gather the stars in,
Who struggled, dancing. The hours counted them
The way shepherds will do it, mornings, in oak shadow,
Numbering their cows and sheep off, before they drive them
To pastureland along the green banks of rivers.

Quand la Lune monstroit sa corne venerable,
   Les Heures de rechef ouvroient la grande estable,
   Où les Astres logeoient en repos tout le jour,
   Les remenant baller du Ciel tout à-l'entour,
   Puis les serroient par compte à l'heure accoustumée
   Que le Soleil avoit nostre terre allumée:
   Si est ce qu'à la fin un estrange malheur
   (Un malheur peut servir) mist leur flamme en valeur,
   La nuict que les Geantz, à toute peine, enterent
   Pelion dessus Osse, & sur Osse planterent
   Le nuageux Olympe, à fin de debouter
   Jupiter de son regne, & vaincu, le donter:
   Les Astres, des ce soir, force & puissance prindrent,
   Et pour jamais au Ciel un lieu ferme retindrent:
   Desja ces grans Geans en grimpant contremont,
   D'Olympe sourcilleux avoient gaigné le front,
   Et ja tenoient le Ciel: & le filz de Saturne
   Eussent emprissonné dans la chartre nocturne
   De l'abysme d'Enfer, où il tient enserrez
   Et de mains, & de piedz, les Titans enferrez:
   Sans l'Astre, qui depuis eut le surnom de l'Ourse,
   Qui regardoit pour lors toute seule la course
   Des autres qui dançoient, & si ne dançoit pas,
   Ayant, comme ja lasse, arresté ses beaux pas
   Fermes devers Borée, & là, voyant l'embuche
   Que brassoient les Geants, tout soudain elle huche
   La troupe de ses Sœurs, & s'en va reciter
   En tramblant l'ambuscade au pere Jupiter.

Armez-vous (dist l'Estoille) armez, vestez vos armes,
   Armez vous, armez vous: je ne sçay quelz gendarmes
   Ont voulu trois grandz montz l'un sur l'autre entasser
   Pour conquerir le Ciel, & pour vous en chasser.
   Adoncques Jupiter, tout en-sursaut commande,
   Ayant sa peau de Chevre, à la celeste bande
   De vestir les harnois, pour garder leur maison,
   Et leurs mains de porter des fers en la prison.

Ja desja s'ataquoit l'escharmouche odieuse,
   Quand des Astres flambans la troupe radieuse
   Pous esbloüir la veüe aux Geantz furieux,
   Se vint droicte planter vis-à-vis de leurs yeux,
   Et alors Jupiter du traict de sa tempeste
   Aux Geantz aveuglez ecarbouilla la teste,

When the moon showed her ancient horn, the hours opened
The doors of the sky stable where the stars had rested
The daylight out, putting them to dance through the entire sky,
And gathered them in again in order at the accustomed time,
After the sun had tinged our earth with live light;
And so it was until a strange useful misfortune
Enhanced their flames.

The giants in one night, operating with force,
Buried Pelion under Ossa, and placed both mountains
Over Olympus's cloudy top, to crush and end
Jupiter's kingdom, master and break the god.
From that evening the stars took on their power
And maintained in the heavens a permanent fixed bastion.
The climbing giants had scaled frowning Olympus, and held
Heaven's frontier; would have made Saturn's son
Their prisoner, in the chasm of hellish
Nightfall, where he had, himself, imprisoned
Bound hand and foot, in irons, his Titan uncles.

The star we have since given the name the Great Bear,
Who singly oversaw the course of dancing of the stars
Who danced—she herself not dancing, for she kept checked
Her graceful gesture, pointing toward the North—she saw there
The giants' planned ambush, and shouted to her sisters;
Rushed, trembling with terror, to tell Jupiter of this trap.

Arm, and take up your weapons, she shouted. Armed men
Have heaped three mountains for the sky's conquering,
And to take your kingdom.

                    Jupiter leaped to command,
Gripping his goatskin buckler. He armed the gods
To hold their mansion: told them to make chains ready.

The enemy attacked, skirmishing. The flaming stars,
Radiant brigade, placed themselves at the raging giants' eyes
And blurred their vision. Jupiter then, with his lightning,
Battered their blinded heads, until the liquid humors
Ran from their eyes, their mouths and nostrils, like new cheese
In its hung basket, that drips drop after drop on the ground.

Leur faisant distiller l'humeur de leurs cerveaux
Par les yeux, par la bouche, & par les deux naseaux,
Comme un fromage mol, qui surpendu s'égoute
Par les trous d'un pannier, à terre goute à goute.

Lors des Astres divins (pour leur peine d'avoir
   Envers Sa Majesté si bien faict leur devoir)
   Aresta la carriere, & tous en telle place
   Qu'ilz avoient de fortune, & en pareille espace,
   D'un lien aimantin leurs plantes attacha,
   Et comme de grans cloux dans le Ciel les ficha,
   Ainsi qu'un mareschal qui hors de la fornaise
   Tire des cloux ardans, tous rayonnez de braise,
   Qu'à grandz coups de marteaux il congne durement
   A-lentour d'une roüe arengez proprement:
   Puis il leur mist es mains le fil des Destinées
   Et leur donna pouvoir sur toutes choses nées,
   Et que par leurs aspectz fatalisé seroit
   Tout cela que Nature en ce monde feroit:
   Retenant toutesfois la superintendence
   A soy, de leurs regardz, & de leur influence,
   Et que, quand il voudroit, tout ce qu'ilz auroient faict
   N'auroit autorité, ny force, ny effect.

Les Estoilles adonc seulles se firent dames
   Sur tous les corps humains, & non dessus les ames,
   Prenant l'Occasion à leur service, à fin
   D'executer çà-bas l'arrest de leur destin.
   Depuis, tous les oyseaux qui volent, & qui chantent,
   Tous les poissons muetz, qui les ondes frequentent,
   Et tous les animaux soit des champs, soit des bois,
   Soit des montz caverneux, furent serfz de leurs loix:
   Mais l'homme, par sur tout, eut sa vie sujette
   Aux destins que le Ciel par les Astres luy jette,
   L'homme, qui le premier comprendre les osa,
   Et telz noms qu'il voulut au Ciel leur composa.
   Ayant percé le cœur de la lance d'Hector,
   L'autre devient Typhis, & veut mener encor'
   Les herôs voir le Phase, & repasser sans crainte
   Des rocz Cyanëans l'emboucheure contrainte,
   Et sçait pronostiquer deux ou trois jours devant,
   Courbé sur le tillac, la tempeste & le vent.

Jupiter, to reward his holy stars, for they
Had done their duty toward him, halted their pointless careenings,
And in the places fortune had led them at that moment,
He held their footsteps in a web of steel,
Leaving the same openings of space between them,
Fixed them into the sky as if they were great nails.

The blacksmith takes his nails, red hot from the embers,
Beats strenuously with his hammer, great blows,
Drives the nails into their proper order on the wheel's rim.

He put the thread of destiny in their hands, then,
Giving them power over all things that are born
So that their fated watching-over may encompass
All nature's doings in the world
He kept to himself the overall governance
Over their influence and their aspects,
So that if He should wish it, none of their plans
Or facts would carry force, authority, or weight.

Since then the stars have made themselves sole mistresses
Over all human bodies; though our souls are free
To take accidents to their service, and try
That way to stop the course of destiny. So, birds
Flying and singing, the mute fish in sea water,
All animals of open land, or of forest,
Of craggy mountain cave, are hostage to their laws.

But man, whose life is subject to the fate heaven
Casts on him, by the stars' doing: man is the first
To dare to know them, and such names as heaven wills on them.

One man devotes himself to war, lives only for pillage,
Seeks death in combat, fighting on the walls of Troy,
His heart skewered on Hector's lance. One becomes Tiphys,
Pilots a boat of heroes to the river's mouth, and fearlessly
Skirts the submerged Cyanean rocks, Colchis's defenders.
Hunched on the deck, he knows how to predict wind
Or storm, two or three days before they arrive.

L'un est né laboureur, & maugré qu'il en aye
   Eguillonne ses bœufz, & fend de mainte playe
   Avec le soc aigu l'eschine des gueréts,
   Pour y semer les dons de la mere Cerés.
   L'autre est né vigneron, & d'une droite ligne
   Dessuz les montz pierreux plante la noble vigne,
   Ou taille les vieux cepz, ou leur beche les piedz,
   Ou rend aux eschallatz les provins mariés.

L'un pesche par contrainte (ainsi vous pleut Estoilles)
   Et conduisant sur l'eau ses rames, & ses voilles,
   Traine son rét maillé, & ose bien armer
   Son bras, pour assommer les monstres de la mer:
   Aucunefois il plonge, & sans reprandre haleine
   Espie les Tritons jusque au fond de l'arene,
   Aucunefois il tend ses friands hameçons,
   Et sur le bord derobe aux fleuves leurs poissons.
   L'autre se fait chasseur, & perd dans son courage
   Le soing de ses enfans, & de tout son mesnage,
   Pour courir par les bois apres quelque sanglier,
   Ou pour faire les loups aux dogues estrangler,
   Et languist s'il n'atache à sa porte les testes,
   Et les diverses peaux de mille estranges bestes.

L'un va dessouz la terre, & fouille les metaux
   D'or, d'argent, & de fer, la semence des maux,
   Que nature n'avoit, comme tressaige mere,
   (Pour nostre grand profit) voulu mettre en lumiere:
   Puis devient alchimiste, et multiplie en vain
   L'or aislé, qui si tost luy vole de la main.
   L'autre par le metier sa navette promeine,
   Ou peigne les toisons d'une grossiere laine,
   Et diriés que d'Arachne il est le nourrisson.
   L'un est graveur, orfevre, entailleur, & maçon,
   Traffiqueur, lapidaire, & mercier, qui va querre
   Des biens, à son peril, en quelque estrange terre.
   Aux autres vous donnez des métiers bien meilleurs,
   Et ne les faictes pas mareschaux, ny tailleurs,
   Mais philosophes grans, qui par longues estudes
   Ont faict un art certain de voz incertitudes:
   Ausquelz avez donné puissance d'escouter
   Voz mysteres divins, pour nous les raconter.

One is born laborer, and for all he's worth
He goads his oxen, and forces furrowing wounds
To break the back of fallow land with the hooked plow
To sow there mother Ceres' given seeds of wheat.
One is born vinegrower, and with his straight tight line
He rows the noble grapevine on stony hillsides,
Prunes the old vine stocks, or cultivates their roots,
Or guides the grafted shoots onto the vine-props.

So also it may please the stars to have one fish,
Travel by oar, or sail over the water
And drag his woven net. He arms himself carefully
To slaughter the sea's monstrous inhabitants.
Sometimes he dives, and without breathing again
Finds tritons lying on the sandy sea bottom.
Or he may gather up his delicate fishhooks
And from their banks steal fish out of the great rivers.

Another makes of himself a hunter. He trades
The supervision of his children and his household
For bravery, and runs through woods after the wild boar,
Or hunts wolves down with strangling mastiffs. He is depressed
Unless he nails the heads and assorted skins
Of a thousand outlandish animals on his door.

One goes under the earth and digs out various metals,
Gold, silver, and iron—iron the seed of evil,
Which nature, like a mother with common sense,
For our protection intended to keep from the light.
Then he becomes alchemist, and vainly multiplies
The winged gold that so speedily flies out of his hand.
One undertakes to weave; or he might card fat wool,
And claim himself spider Arachne's descendant.
Then there are draftsmen, jewelers, sculptors, masons,
Traveling salesmen, lapidaries, and merchants
Who go, at their peril, to search for benefits in strange lands.
You give happier professions to some others,
Making them neither blacksmiths nor tailors,
But great philosophers, who, by long study,
Have certified by art certain of your vagaries:
For you have given them the power to listen
And then to tell us of your holy mysteries.

Cettuy cy congnoit bien des oyseaux le langage,
   Et sçait conjecturer des songes le presage,
   Il nous dit nostre vie, & d'un propos obscur,
   A qui l'en interrogue annonce le futur.
   Cestuy là des naissance est faict sacré poëte,
   Et jamais souz ses doigs sa Lyre n'est müette,
   Qu'il ne chante tousjours d'un vers melodieux
   Les hymnes excellens des hommes, & des Dieux,
   Ainsi que toy, Mellin, orné de tant de graces,
   Qui en cest art gentil les mieux disans surpasses.

Cestuy-cy plus ardant, & d'un cœur plus hautain
   Guide une colonie en un païs lointain,
   Et n'y a ny torrent, ny mont qui le retienne:
   Ores il faict razer une ville ancienne,
   Ores une nouvelle il bastit de son nom,
   Et ne veut amasser tresor, que de renom.
   Cettuy-là faict le brave, & s'ose faire croire
   Que la hauteur du Ciel il hurte de sa gloire,
   Presque adoré du peuple, & ne veut endurer
   Qu'un autre à luy se vienne en credit mesurer:
   Mais il voit à la fin son audace coupée,
   Et meurt pauvre & fuitif comme un autre Pompée.
   Cettuy comme un Cesar apres avoir rué
   L'Empire sous ses piedz, est à la fin tué
   De ses gens, & ne peut fuïr la destinée
   Certaine, qu'en naissant vous luy avez donnée.
   Sans plus vous nous causez nos biens & nos malheurs,
   Mais vous causez aussi noz diverses humeurs,
   Vous nous faictes ardans, flumatiques, colores,
   Rassis, impatiens, courtisans, solitaires,
   Tristes, plaisans, gentilz, hardis, froidz, orguilleux,
   Eloquens, ignorans, simples, & cauteleux.

Que diray plus de vous? par voz bornes marquées
   Le Soleil refranchist ses courses revoquées,
   Et nous refaict les mois, les ans, & les saisons,
   Selon qu'il entre ou sort de voz belles maisons;
   Dessous vostre pouvoir s'asseurent les grands villes:
   Vous nous donnez des temps les signes tresutilles,
   Et soit que vous couchez, ou soit que vous levez,
   En diverses façons les signes vous avez
   Imprimez sur le front, des vens & des orages,
   Des pluyes, des frimatz, des gresles, & des neiges,

Another understands the languages of birds
And knows how to interpret the meaning of dreams.
He explains our lives to us, and predicts the future.
Another, from his birth, is made a holy poet
Whose lyre speaks constantly under his fingers;
Whose songlike poems sing hymns of God and good men
As do yourself, Melin. You are made graceful
In this art, and gentle, above all others who speak.

One eager man, high-hearted, leads a colony
Into a distant land, held back by neither mountain
Nor rushing river. He destroys ancient cities,
Builds new ones which he blesses with his own name,
His treasure lust being subdued to lust for glory.
One does brave deeds and lets himself believe heaven itself
High as it is, is threatened by his daring glory.
He has the adoration of the people. He endures
No challenger's arising who might test his value.
His finish finds his daring cut back badly for him.
His death is poverty-stricken, fugitive, like Pompey's.
One is a Caesar. He has trampled his empire
Under his feet, and his own citizens kill him.
That is his finish, his destiny inescapable,
Your certain gift, given as he came from the womb.

You cause our fortunes and misfortunes. Your burning makes
Our diverse characters as well, our chemical balance.
You make us eager or weary, angry, sedate,
Impatient, diplomatic, solitary, sad,
Pleasant or graceful, hardy, cold, conceited,
Eloquent, ignorant, gullible, or cunning.

I will say this more of you. By your marked boundaries
The sun swings back the shifting of its course again
And makes its repeated patterns of months, years and seasons.
As he enters or comes out of your lovely houses,
Under your power whole cities are warranted.
Your ascent and descendance give sign of the weather.
The signs marked on your faces herald wind and storm.
Rain, frost, hail, snow. The colors your flames exhibit
Let us know if our days will be clear or heavy.

Et selon les couleurs qui paignent voz flambeaux,
On congnoit si les jours seront ou laidz ou beaux.
Vous nous donnez aussi par voz marques celestes
Les presages certains des fiebvres & des pestes,
Et des maux, qui bien tost doivent tomber çà bas,
Les signes de famine, & des futurs combas:
Car vous estes de Dieu les sacrez caracteres,
Ainçois de ce grand Dieu fidelles secretaires,
Par qui sa volunté faict sçavoir aux humains,
Comme s'il nous marquoit un papier de ses mains.
Non seulement par vous ce grand Seigneur & Maistre
Donne ses volontez aux hommes à congnoistre:
Mais par l'onde & par l'air & par le feu trespront,
Voire (qui le croira) par les lignes qui sont
Escrites dans noz mains, & sur nostre visage,
Desquelles qui pourroit au vray sçavoir l'usage,
Nous verrions imprimez clairement là dedans
Ensemble noz mauvais & noz bons accidens:
Mais faute de pouvoir telles lignes entendre,
Qui sont propres à nous, nous ne povons comprendre
Ce que Dieu nous escrit, & sans jamais prevoir
Nostre malheur futur, tousjours nous laissons cheoir
Apres une misere, en une autre misere:
Mais certes par sur tous en vous reluit plus claire
La volonté de Dieu, d'autant que sa grandeur
Alume de plus pres vostre belle splendeur.

O que loing de raison celuy follement erre
    Qui dit que vous paissez des humeurs de la terre!
Si l'humeur vous paissoit, vous seriés corrompuz,
Et pource, Astres divins, vous n'estes point repuz,
Vostre feu vous nourrist, ainsi qu'une fontaine
Qui tant plus va coulant, plus se regorge plaine,
Comme ayant de son eau le surjon perennel:
Ainsi, ayant en vous le surjon eternel
D'un feu natif, jamais ne vous faut la lumiere,
Laquelle luit en vous, comme au Soleil, premiere.

Your heavenly signals give us clear warning
Of plagues and fevers, and of the other calamities
Which are about to fall: famines, approaching warfare.
For you are God's sacred written language, God's
Faithful secretaries, through whom His will is made known
To us, as if He had written on paper with His own hands.

Our overlord, our master, gives us some understanding
Not only through the stars, of his willed happenings,
But by the movements of air, water and nimble fire,
By the lines marked on our hands and on our faces,
Which one who has true knowledge can make out clearly
And read the fortune or misfortune intended for us.
But beyond knowing what these lines intend, which are
Our individual markings, we cannot learn
What God has written. And without some forewarning
Of boding trouble, we will consistently stumble
Out of one misery into another misery.
This is steadfast. God's will shines clearly in your light.
His glory glows more brightly near your lovely splendor.

It is folly born of ignorance that leads some
To say you feast on the earth's liquids. If you fed
On our waters, you would become corrupted;
And therefore, holy stars, you are not to be fed:
But nourished by your fire, the way a fresh water spring
Brims and overflows, runs flowing, since it exists
Out of a permanent source of water, continually.
In the same way, in you, an eternal native fire
Springs, and is the source of unfailing light. The light
The sun burned with at the beginning shines in you.

The smallest of you is larger than the earth is.
How could the earth's gripped liquid give sustenance enough,
Or rise to touch you, passing from this low ground,
Without being dried out by the rays of the sun
Before it reached your height? And they are fools, also,
Who think you mortal, dying with us, born with us;
Think the most brilliant are reserved to the destinies of kings,
The least lively are set aside for poor people.

Fol est encore celuy, qui mortelz vous pense estre,
    Mourir quand nous mourons, & quand nous naissons, naistre,
    Et que les plus luisans aux Roys sont destinez,
    Et les moins flamboyans aux Paovres assignez:
    Tel soing ne vous tient pas, car apres noz naissances
    Que vous avez versé dedans nous voz puissances,
    Plus ne vous chaut de nous, ny de noz faictz aussi:
    Ains courez en repoz, delivrez de soucy,
    Et francz des passions, qui des le berceau suyvent
    Les hommes qui ça-bas chargez de peine vivent.

Je vous salue, Enfans de la premiere nuit,
    Heureux Astres divins, par qui tout se conduit:
    Pendant que vous tournez vostre dance ordonnée
    Au Ciel, j'acompliray, çà-bas la destinée
    Qu'il vous pleut me verser, bonne ou maivaise, alors
    Que mon ame immortelle entra dedans mon corps.

Pain does not live in you. After we have been born,
When you have poured our powers into us, you have
No further responsibility for us, our doings;
But restful, secure from hardships, innocent of passion,
You witness us from our cradles. It is our lives that are painful.

You are the children of the earliest nightfall,
Blessed, holy stars: the governors of all that moves:
As long as you turn the ordered figures of your dancing
In the sky, I will fulfill my destiny here
As you have pleased to give it, whether good or ill,
Since the immortal soul first came into my body.

26. ODELETTE

Les espics sont à Cerés,
    Aus Chevrepieds les forés,
    A Clore l'herbe nouvelle,
    A Phebus le verd laurier,
    A Minerve l'olivïer.
    Et le beau pin à Cybelle.

Aus Zefires le dous bruit,
    A Pommone le dous fruit
    L'onde aus Ninfes est sacrée,
    A Flore les belles fleurs,
    Mais les soucis & les pleurs
    Sont sacrés à Cytherée.

for Maizie

Wheat's ear is Ceres',
The forests to the goatish gods.
To Chloris new grass;
Green laurel, Apollo's;
Cybele's, pine.

Soft sounds, the Zephyrs';
Pomona's all sweet fruit.
Water is sacred to nymphs,
Flowers to Flora.
But tears and sadness
Are sacred to Cythera.

27.

Le vingtiesme d'Avril couché sur l'herbelette,
    Je vy ce me sembloit, en dormant un Chevreuil,
    Qui çà, qui là marchoit où le menoit son vueil,
    Foulant les belles fleurs de mainte gambelette.

Une corne et une autre encore nouvelette
    Enfloit son petit front d'un gracieux orgueil:
    Comme un Soleil luisoit la rondeur de son œil,
    Et un carquan pendoit sous sa gorge douillette.

Si tost que je le vy, je voulu courre apres,
    Et luy qui m'avisa, print sa fuite ès forests,
    Où se mocquant de moy, ne me voulut attendre:

Mais en suivant son trac, je ne m'avisay pas
    D'un piege entre les fleurs, qui me lia les pas;
    Ainsi pour prendre autruy, moymesme me feis prendre.

The twentieth of April. This dream: I had been
Sleeping outdoors. A doe, trampling flowers
With her delicate wayward legs.

She was a young one, the two buds on her forehead
Just swelling into horns, gracefully: her eyes
Bursting with light, reflected sun light.

A ring hung on her narrow throat.

I wanted to run for her. She saw that, and took
Flight into the trees, teasing, egging me on.

My eyes on her track, I was not watching for the snare
Concealed in flowers, that caught my feet: my own
Net spread to tangle her took me in.

28.

Marie, levez-vous, ma jeune paresseuse,
    Ja la gaye Alouette au ciel a fredonné,
    Et ja le Rossignol doucement jargonné
    Dessus l'espine assis, sa complainte amoureuse.

Sus debout allon voir l'herbelette perleuse,
    Et vostre beau rosier de boutons couronné,
    Et vos œillets mignons, ausquels aviez donné
    Hier au soir de l'eau d'une main si songneuse.

Harsoir en vous couchant vous jurastes voz yeux
    D'estre plus-tost que moy ce matin esveillée:
    Mais le dormir de l'Aube aux filles gracieux

Vous tient d'un doux sommeil la paupiere sillée.
    Je vais baiser voz yeux et vostre beau tetin
    Cent fois pour vous apprendre à vous lever matin.

Get up, you sluggish creature: Mary,
The lark has set the entire sky to shaking.
The nightingale has done his jargoning,
Perched on his thorn.

The water you put so carefully on the pinks in the evening
Already blossoms back as morning light. Stand up.
We'll shatter the cold pearls on the grass,
The buttons of mist silvering the buds on the rose bushes: and look,

When you took to your bed, you swore your eyes
Would open before mine, but the dawn's sleep has touched
Your hooded eyes with graceful sleeping.

I kiss them, and your little breast.
Wake up. I'll teach you.

29.

J'ay desiré cent fois me transformer, et d'estre
   Un esprit invisible, afin de me cacher
   Au fond de vostre cœur, pour l'humeur rechercher
   Qui vous fait contre moy si cruelle apparoistre.

Si j'estois dedans vous, au moins je serois maistre
   De l'humeur qui vous fait contre l'Amour pecher,
   Et si n'auriez ny pouls, ny nerfs dessous la chair,
   Que je ne recherchasse à fin de vous cognoistre.

Je sçaurois maugré vous et voz complexions,
   Toutes voz volontez, et voz conditions,
   Et chasserois si bien la froideur de voz veines,

Que les flames d'Amour vous y allumeriez:
   Puis quand je les voirrois de son feu toutes pleines,
   Je me referois homme, et lors vous m'aimeriez.

I want to be inside you—to be transformed
Into invisible soul, and hide myself
In the pit of your heart, to convert your humor.

I would become the master of your emotion.
I would discover your pulse, the nerves' tracks through your flesh,
And change your disdain. Or at least I would know you,

In spite of yourself, against your will.
I would be party to your desires, and your terms.

And I would chase the chill from your veins
So perfectly, love could send fire in.

Then, when I saw them brim full of flame
I would step out and be a man again.

30.

Vous mesprisez nature: estes vous si cruelle
    De ne vouloir aimer? voyez les Passereaux
    Qui demenent l'amour, voyez les Colombeaux,
    Regardez la Ramier, voyez la Tourterelle:

Voyez deçà delà d'une fretillante aile
    Voleter par les bois les amoureux oiseaux,
    Voyez la jeune vigne embrasser les ormeaux,
    Et toute chose rire en la saison nouvelle.

Icy la bergerette en tournant son fuseau
    Desgoise ses amours, et là le pastoureau
    Respond à sa chanson, icy toute chose aime:

Tout parle de l'amour, tout s'en veut enflamer:
    Seulement vostre cœur froid d'une glace extreme
    Demeure opiniastre, et ne veut point aimer.

You despise common nature. Cruelty
Occupies your ability to love. All around you, birds—
Doves and wild pigeons, sparrows—
Are frantic with winged coupling: and you see it.

Their crazed wings hurl birds leaping past branches,
Love struck. The young vine grips the elm.
Laughter rides all in this new, this amazed season.

Everything else here is in love. The laborer trades songs
With the girl whose affections babble innocently
While her spindle works; and the words and the work

Move all to the point of heat that begs release in flame.
All but your heart, whose ice has yet to crack:
Stubborn, unyielding, hidebound, headstrong, will not love me.

31. CHANSON

Je veux chanter en ces vers ma tristesse:
 Car autrement chanter je ne pourrois,
 Veu que je suis absent de ma maistresse:
 Si je chantois autrement, je mourrois.

Pour ne mourir il faut donc que je chante
 En chants piteux ma plaintive langueur,
 Pour le départ de ma maistresse absente,
 Qui de mon sein m'a desrobé le cœur.

Desja l'Esté, et Ceres la blêtiere,
 Ayant le front orné de son present,
 Ont ramené la moisson nourriciere
 Depuis le temps que d'elle suis absent,

Loin de ses yeux dont la lumiere belle
 Seule pourroit guarison me donner:
 Et si j'estois là bas en la nacelle,
 Me pourroit faire au monde retourner.

Mais ma raison est si bien corrompue
 Par une fausse imagination,
 Que nuict et jour je la porte en la veuë,
 Et sans la voir j'en ay la vision.

Comme celuy qui contemple les nues,
 Fantastiquant mille monstres bossus,
 Hommes, oiseaux, et Chimeres cornues,
 Tant par les yeux nos esprits sont deceus.

Et comme ceux, qui d'une haleine forte,
 En haute mer, à puissance de bras
 Tirent la rame, ils l'imaginent torte,
 Et toutefois la rame ne l'est pas:

Now I will sing about being sad.
There is no other singing open to me
Her absence makes this so, and makes my absence.
I must sing sadness or die,

Must die or sing my sadness
At her going; at the wound
Left where my heart was taken.

Summer gone, Ceres the wheat woman
Striding in a haze of golden chaff,
Has brought our harvest back.
And she is absent still.

Her eyes could heal me; even
If I were huddled in the boat for Hell,
Could bring me back.

My intelligence is made corrupt
By the vacant imagining that throws her vision
On empty days and the false nights.

I am like a man staring at clouds,
Contriving hunchbacks, monsters, men,
Birds and winged beasts, Our minds
Are twisted out of reason by our eyes.

Like a man perched on the peak of a wave,
Who bends his arm to pull with all the power he can,
And finding empty air, loses his oars.

The loveliness I look for
Has left its portrait pasted on my eyes.
I can see nothing real.

Ainsi je voy d'une œillade trompée
    Cette beauté, dont je suis depravé,
    Qui par les yeux dedans l'ame frapée,
    M'a vivement son portrait engravé.

Et soit que j'erre au plus haut des montaignes
    Ou dans un bois, loing de gens et de bruit,
    Soit au rivage, ou parmy les campaignes,
    Tousjours à l'œil ce beau portrait me suit,

Si j'apperçoy quelque champ qui blondoye
    D'espics frisez au travers des sillons,
    Je pense voir ses beaux cheveux de soye
    Espars au vent en mille crespillons.

Si le Croissant au premier mois j'avise,
    Je pense voir son sourcil ressemblant
    A l'arc d'un Turc, qui la sagette a mise
    Dedans la coche, et menace le blanc.

Quand à mes yeux les estoiles drillantes
    Viennent la nuict en temps calme s'offrir,
    Je pense voir ses prunelles ardantes,
    Que je ne puis ny fuyr, ny souffrir.

Quand j'apperçoy la rose sur l'espine,
    Je pense voir de ses lèvres le teint:
    La rose au soir de sa couleur decline,
    L'autre couleur jamais ne se desteint.

Quand j'apperçoy les fleurs en quelque prée
    Ouvrir leur grace au lever du Soleil,
    Je pense voir de sa face pourprée
    S'espanouyr le beau lustre vermeil.

Si j'apperçoy quelque chesne sauvage,
    Qui jusqu'au ciel éleve ses rameaux,
    Je pense voir sa taille et son corsage,
    Ses pieds, sa greve, et ses coudes jumeaux.

Si j'entends bruire une fontaine claire,
    Je pense ouyr sa voix dessus le bord,
    Qui, se plaignant de ma triste misere,
    M'appelle à soy pour me donner confort.

I carry her image wandering in the mountains,
In woodlands, amongst quiet farms
After men and their noise have left them.

Wheat ripens in its field,
The fringing blades, blond above plowed furrows.
I think her hair shivers there in the wind like crimped silk.

Or the curved edge of the moon
Could be her brow, a turk's bent bow,
Its arrow couched, menacing the eye.

When clear night stares me down with stars
It could be her eyes burning there
Beyond my power.

The rose in its thicket, her mouth
Whose color fades with evening—the roses fade,
Not she.

Field flowers, opening to the sun's touch:
Her face tinged with its crimson,
Blossoming.

The wild oak hauls its branches to the sky:
Her graceful body, limbs, the bend of her arm.

Her voice tumbles in clear streams on stones
Where I call water to take my council, and learn
The shape of my sadness, to bring me comfort.

I keep melancholy. The world
And I are printed with the same fantastic forms,
Her hundred beauties.

Love is the fury of an outraged fantasy.
It has been well defined in medical literature
As illness medicine fails to relieve.

The healing of this disease can be nothing but grief.
I would do better to keep fire in my veins,
Or to attract the plague.

Voila comment pour estre fantastique,
    En cent façons ses beautez j'apperçoy,
    Et m'esjouis d'estre melancholique,
    Pour recevoir tant de formes en moy.

Aimer vrayment est une maladie,
    Les medecins la sçavent bien juger,
    Nommant Amour fureur de fantaisie,
    Qui ne se peut par herbes soulager.

J'aimerois mieux la fièvre dans mes veines,
    Ou quelque peste, ou quelqu'autre douleur,
    Que de souffrir tant d'amoureuses peines,
    Dont le bon-heur n'est sinon que malheur.

Or va, Chanson, dans le sein de Marie,
    Pour l'asseurer, que ce n'est tromperie
    Des visions que je raconte icy,
    Qui me font vivre et mourir en soucy.

My song should go and find the hollow
Between Mary's breasts, and rest there.
Let her know I suffer from careful visions.
Let her see the realness here, to keep, and to assure her:
My life and death are painful.

32. ODE

Dieu vous gard, messagers fidelles
    Du printemps, gentes Arondelles,
    Huppes, Coqs, Rousignolets,
    Tourtres, & vous oyseaus sauvages
    Qui de cent sortes de ramages
    Animez les bois verdelets:

Dieu vous gard, belles Paquerettes,
    Belles Rozes, belles fleurettes
    De Mars, & vous boutons cognuz
    Du sang d'Ajax & de Narcisse,
    Et vous Thyn, Anis & Melisse,
    Vous soyez les tresbien venuz.

Dieu vous gard, troupe diaprée
    Des Papillons, qui par la prée
    Les douces herbes suçotez,
    Et vous nouvel essain d'abeilles,
    Qui les fleurs jaunes & vermeilles
    Indifferemment baisotez.

Cent mille fois je resalüe
    Vostre belle & douce venüe.
    O que j'ayme cette saison,
    Et ce doux quaquet des rivages,
    Au prix des vents & des orages
    Qui m'enfermoient en la maison!

for Sadie

God grace you, faithful messengers,
Spring's quick swallows,
Hoopoe, cuckoo, nightingale,
Doves and you wild birds
Whose hundred singings
Shake the woods.

God grace you, daisies
Lovely, lovely roses, lovely
Violets; and buds once stained
By blood of Ajax; narcissus;
Thyme; anise and lemon balm:
That you be welcome.

God grace you, dappled
Troops of butterflies
Who suck sweet grasses in the fields;
New swarms of bees
Who graze your mouths in yellow,
In bright crimson flowers.

This graceful fair arrival
Takes my greeting, these thousand
Greetings; for I love
This season, these
Chitterings of streamsides,
For which I paid no more than this:
My being housebound during storms,
During the winter's wind.

33. A SON LIVRE

Mon fils, si tu sçavois ce qu'on dira de toy,
  Tu ne voudrois jamais desloger de chez moy,
  Enclos en mon estude: et ne voudrois te faire
  Salir ny fueilleter aux mains du populaire.
  Quand tu seras party, sans jamais retourner,
  Estranger loin de moy te faudra sejourner:
  » Car ainsi que le vent sans retourner s'en-vole,
  » Sans espoir de retour s'eschappe la parole.

Or tu es ma parole, à qui de nuict et jour
  J'ay conté les propos que m'enseignoit Amour,
  Pour les mettre en ces vers qu'en lumiere tu portes,
  Crochetant, maugré moy, de mon bufet les portes,
  Pauvret! qui ne sçais pas que nos peuples se font
  Plus subtilz par le nez que le Rhinoceront.

Donc, avant que tenter le hazard du naufrage,
  Voy du port la tempeste, et demeure au rivage:
  Trop tard on se repent, quand on s'est embarqué.
  Tu seras assez tost les mesdisans mocqué
  D'yeux, et de haussebecs, et d'un branler de teste.
  Sage est celuy qui croit à qui bien l'admonneste.

Tu sçais (mon cher enfant) que je ne te voudrois
  Ny tromper ny mocquer: laschement je faudrois,
  Comme un Tygre engendré de farouche nature,
  Si je voulois trahir ma propre geniture.
  Car tel que je te voy, n'agueres je te fis
  Et je ne t'aime moins qu'un pere aime son fils.

*   *   *

for my parents

Son, if you knew how you will be talked of
You would keep the safety of my quiet walls,
Not want to move out of the house.
People crease words like paper.
Your going cannot be taken back.
You will become estranged.
Words spoken are as lost
As the blown wind.
I have placed private judgments,
Love's teachings, in my verses here,
Which are my word. I feel
Almost betrayed by daylight on them, as if
By their own act, they'd picked my locks and escaped.

Poor fool, you don't yet understand
The compassion and the subtlety of the public
Rivals that of the rhinoceros.

You'd stand on the wharf, looking seaward at squalls,
And decide to wait before putting to sea, wouldn't you?
It's late to turn back when you're breathing salt water.

They'll wink, make mocking jokes, shrug,
Shake their heads.
You would have been wise to heed my warnings.

I love you no less than I would my son,
And would not wish shame, nor mockery, on you,
For this becoming public.

Non, non, je ne veux pas que pour ce livre icy
    J'entre dans un escolle, ou qu'un regent aussy
    Me lise pour parade: il suffit si m'amie
    Le touche de la main dont elle tient ma vie.
    Car je suis satisfait, si elle prend à gré
    Ce labeur que je vouë à ses pieds consacré,
    Et à celles qui sont de nature amiables,
    Et qui jusq'à mort ne sont point variables.

I did not intend this book as my ticket to college,
Or that some tenured scholar show off at its expense.
If my lover will touch it
(My life is in her hand)
I am content to set my labor at her feet.
The book is made for her; and it is for you, also,
Who are by nature friendly, and will defend what you find valuable.

34.

D'un sang froid, noir, et lent, je sens glacer mon cœur,
  Quand quelcun parle à vous, ou quand quelcun vous touche:
  Une ire autour du cœur me dresse l'escarmouche,
  Jaloux contre celuy qui reçoit tant d'honneur.

Je suis (je n'en mens point) jaloux de vostre sœur,
  De mon ombre, de moy, de mes yeux, de ma bouche:
  Ainsi ce petit Dieu qui la raison me bousche,
  Me tient tousjours en doute, en soupson, et en peur.

Je ne puis aimer ceux, à qui vous faites chere,
  Fussent ils mes cousins, mes oncles, et mon frere:
  Je maudis leurs faveurs, j'abhorre leur bon-heur.

Les amans et les Roys de compagnons ne veulent.
  S'ils en ont de fortune, en armes ils s'en deulent.
  Avoir un compagnon, c'est avoir un Seigneur.

If someone speaks to you, or touches
Your body, I feel my heart slowly
Go cold, and cover with black blood.

Anger surrounds my brain with skirmishing.
It is jealousy that anyone should be so honored.

Doubt, fear, suspicion, clog my reason along with my affection.
I am jealous of your sister, my shadow, my eyes, my mouth even.

I cannot love those to whom you show affection,
Be they my cousins, uncles—be it my brother even—
I resent their good will, and hate their well-being.

Lovers and kings want no companions.
Good fortune's comrades won't arm to defend you.
Companions become masters.

35.

Marie, baisez moy: non: ne me baisez pas,
    Mais tirez moy le cœur de vostre douce haleine:
    Non: se le tirez pas, mais hors de chaque veine
    Succez moy toute l'ame esparse entre voz bras:

Non: ne la succez pas: car apres le trespas
    Que serois-je, sinon une semblance vaine,
    Sans corps de sur la rive, où l'amour ne demeine
    Comme il fait icy haut, qu'en feintes ses esbas?

Pendant que nous vivons, entr'aimons nous, Marie,
    Amour ne regne point sur la troupe blesmie
    Des morts, qui sont sillez d'un long somme de fer.

C'est abus que Pluton ait aimé Prosperpine,
    Si doux soing n'entre point en si dure poitrine:
    Amour regne en la terre, et non point en enfer.

Mary, kiss me: no: don't kiss me,
But drag my heart out with your sweet breathing.
Not drag—but from each vein suck out
My scattered soul between your arms.

Not suck: my life lost
What would I be but a vain image,
Bodiless, on that bank where love
Lives no more, as it does here,
But fakes at frolic.

While we are living we must love each other.
Love does not rule the pale crowd
Of the dead, plowed into iron sleep.

It is a lie Pluto loved Proserpina.
His attention was not mild, nor careful.
Hell has no love in it. Love
Rules the earth, the living.

36. LE VOYAGE DE TOURS OU LES AMOUREUX
THOINET ET PERROT.

C'estoit en la saison que l'amoureuse Flore
    Faisoit pour son amy les fleurettes esclorre
    Par les prez bigarrez d'autant d'esmail de fleurs,
    Que le grand arc du ciel s'esmaille de couleurs:
    Lors que les papillons et les blondes avettes,
    Les uns chargez au bec, les autres aux cuissettes,
    Errent par les jardins, et les petits oiseaux
    Voletans par les bois de rameaux en rameaux
    Amassent la bechée, et parmy la verdure
    Ont soucy comme nous de leur race future.

Thoinet au mois d'Avril passant par Vandomois,
    Me mena voir à Tours Marion que j'aimois,
    Qui aux nopces estoit d'une sienne cousine:
    Et ce Thoinet aussi alloit voir sa Francine,
    Que Venus enfonçant un trait plein de rigueur,
    Luy avoit d'une playe escrite dans le cœur.

Nous partismes tous deux du hameau de Coustures,
    Nous passasmes Gastine et ses hautes verdures,
    Nous passasmes Marré, et vismes à my-jour
    Du pasteur Phelipot s'eslever la grand tour,
    Qui de Beaumont la Ronse honore le village,
    Comme un pin fait honneur aux arbres d'un bocage.
    Ce pasteur qu'on nommoit Phelippot tout gaillard,
    Chez luy nous festoya jusques au soir bien tard.
    De là vinsmes coucher au gué de Lengenrie,
    Sous les saules plantez le long d'une prairie:
    Puis dés le poinct du jour redoublant le marcher,
    Nous vismes dans un bois s'eslever le clocher
    De sainct Cosme pres Tours, où la nopce gentille
    Dans un pré se faisoit au beau milieu de l'isle.

for Julia Norris

Flora was in her fancy in that season,
And kindled flowers for her lover
Through the bright speckled fields,
More colors than the great sky's bow can bend.
Butterflies and pollen blonded bees
Mouth charged, thigh bursting,
Wandered through gardens. Small birds
Darted through woods from branch to branch
With squirming beaksfull, caring amongst green leaves
For their own children, as we care for ours.

April. Thoinet, who was passing through Vendome
Took me to Tours, to visit Marion, whom I loved,
Who had arrived there for a cousin's wedding;
Thoinet intending also to visit his Francine,
Venus having carved her name
In the bark of his heart, and pretty deeply.

We left the little hamlet of Coutures,
Passed through the tall green arches of Gastine,
Passed through Marré, and by noontime
Had made Beaumont la Ronce, whose tower
The shepherd Phellipot built to honor it
As a pine honors a grove of trees.
This grand fellow, Phellipot,
Feasted us late into the evening
And we went on to sleep at the ford of Lengenrie
Under the planted ranks of willows at the meadow's edge.
From dawn on we made better time,
Came to the woods from which the clock tower
Of St. Côme, near Tours, rises:
And the marriage was already underway
In the glade at the island's heart.

Là Francine dansoit, de Thoinet le soucy,
   Là Marion balloit, qui fut le mien aussy:
   Puis nous mettans tous deux en l'ordre de la dance,
   Thoinet tout le premier ceste plainte commence.
Ma Francine, mon cœur, qu'oublier je ne puis . . .

*   *   *

Je suis, s'il t'en souvient, Thoinet, qui dés jeunesse
   Te voyant sur le Clain t'appella sa maistresse,
   Qui musette et flageol à ses lévres usa
   Pour te donner plaisir, mais cela m'abusa:
   Car te pensant fléchir comme une femme humaine,
   Je trouvay ta poitrine et ton aureille pleine,
   Helas qui l'eust pensé! de cent mille glassons
   Lesquels ne t'ont permis d'escouter mes chansons:
   Et toutesfois le temps, qui les prez de leurs herbes
   Despouille d'an en an, et les champs de leurs gerbes,
   Ne m'a point despouillé le souvenir du jour
   Ny du mois où je mis en tes yeux mon amour:
   Ny ne fera jamais, voire eusse-je avallée
   L'onde qui court là bas sous l'obscure valée.

C'estoit au mois d'Avril, Francine, il m'en souvient,
   Quand tout arbre florit, quand la terre devient
   De vieillesse en jouvance, et l'estrange arondelle
   Fait contre un soliveau sa maison naturelle:
   Quand la Lymace au dos qui porte sa maison,
   Laisse un trac sur les fleurs: quand la blonde toison
   Va couvrant la chenille, et quand parmy les prées
   Volent les papillons aux ailes diaprées,
   Lors que fol je te vy, et depuis je n'ay peu
   Rien voir apres tes yeux que tout ne m'ait despleu.

*   *   *

O ma belle Francine, ô ma fiere, et pourquoy
   En dansant, de tes mains ne me prends tu le doy?
   Pourquoi lasse du bal entre ses fleurs couchée,
   N'ay-je sur ton giron ou la teste panchée,

Francine (Thoinet's hardship) was dancing;
Marion dancing too—she being mine;
And so the two of us joined in the dance
In order: Thoinet, taking the lead, began to
Complain to her.

Francine, my heart, as if I could forget you:

Don't you recall Thoinet, who called you his sweet lover
When I first saw you, young, on the Clain river,
And played the pipes to give you pleasure?
But that dismays me;
For thinking to touch you like a human female
I find your heart and ear filled up already.
Who would have thought it? When I could have spent my songs
More profitably, courting drift ice.
Though years strip pastures of their green time after time,
Take sheaves from wheat fields;
I have not lost the memory of the day,
Of the whole month,
I placed my love before your eyes:
Nor would I, even if I drank
The black wave running in the shadowed valley.

Francine, I remember it was the month of April,
The trees in flower, the aged earth
Growing young again; the swallows
Back from foreign parts, making their natural homes
Under the eaves. The snail, backpacking his house,
Trailed through the flowers; its blond pelt
Covered the caterpillar; throughout the fields
Butterflies, with their mottled wings
Were flying. I saw you, and went almost foolish
With it. And since then, since seeing your eyes,
Nothing else could please mine.

Ou mes yeux sur les tiens, ou la lévre dessus
Tes tetins relevez comme gazons bossus?
Te semblay-je trop vieil? encor la barbe tendre
Ne fait que commencer sur ma joüe à s'estendre,
Et ta bouche qui passe en beauté le coural,
S'elle veut me baiser, ne se fera point mal:
Mais ainsi qu'un Lezard se cache sous l'herbette,
Sous ma blonde toison cacheras ta languette:
Puis en la retirant, tu tireras à toy
Mon cœur pour te baiser, qui sortira de moy.

*   *   *

O belle au doux regard, Francine au beau sourcy,
Baise moy, je te prie, et m'embrasses ainsy
Qu'un arbre est embrassé d'une vigne bien forte.
« Souvent un vain baiser quelque plaisir apporte.
Je meurs! tu me feras despecer ce bouquet,
Que j'ay cueilly pour toy, de Thin et de Muguet,
Et de la rouge-fleur qu'on nomme Cassandrette,
Et de la blanche-fleur qu'on appelle Olivette,
A qui Bellot donna et la vie et le nom,
Et de celle qui prend de ton nom son surnom.

Las! où fuis tu de moy? ha ma fiere ennemie,
Je m'en vois despouiller jaquette et souquenie,
Et m'en courray tout nud au haut de ce rocher,
Où tu vois ce garçon à la ligne pescher,
Afin de me lancer à corps perdu dans Loire,
Pour laver mon soucy, ou afin de tant boire
D'escumes et de flots, que la flamme d'aimer
Par l'eau contraire au feu se puisse consumer.

Ainsi disoit Thoinet, qui se pasma sur l'herbe,
Presque transi de voir sa dame si superbe,
Qui rioit de son mal, sans daigner seulement
D'un seul petit clin d'œil appaiser son tourment.

J'ouvrois desja la lévre apres Thoinet, pour dire
De combien Marion m'estoit encores pire,
Quand j'avise sa mere en haste gaigner l'eau,
Et sa fille emmener avec elle au bâteau,

Tired of dancing, now, we could rest in these flowers,
My head rest in your lap, my eyes on yours;
Your breasts heaved grassy hummocks; and my lips
Rest on your nipple.
Could I seem so much too old to you?
The beard I've started on my cheek is tender still.
Your mouth is lovelier than coral. If it likes
To kiss me, it would do itself no harm
The way a lizard hides under the grass
You'd snake your little tongue into my blond beard
And draw the heart back,
Which would come gladly out of me to kiss you.

Francine, with the neat bent brow and gentle gaze,
I beg you, kiss me, let your arms circle me
As a tree stands wrapped in the strong vine.
Sometimes a heedless kiss brings pleasure.
I am dying. You'll make me tear the flowers I gathered for you,
Thyme, and lily of the valley, red Cassandra;
White Olivette, so named by Bellot, and so by him invented;
And that whose name is your name.
Where will your vicious pride run from me? Oh,
I'm going to strip off jacket and overalls
And, naked, run up to the cliff top
Where that boy sits with his fishing rod,
And cast myself into the Loire, wash sadness off,
Drink so much froth and ripple
Love's fire can be consumed by its contrary water.
Thoinet spoke so, and collapsed on the ground
Almost transfixed to see his woman's pride
Laugh at his illness; she deigning not even
One wink to assuage his torment.

I had just opened my mouth to speak
After Thoinet, Marion's greater hardship on me,
When I saw her mother hastily take to the water
Dragging her daughter with her, in a punt
That had been waiting for its large charge
And frisking at its tether, the huge trunk
Of a heady willow.

Qui se joüant sur l'onde attendoit ceste charge,
Lié contre le tronc d'un saule au feste large.

Ja les rames tiroient le bâteau bien pansu,
  Et la voile en enflant son grand reply bossu
  Emportoit le plaisir qui mon cœur tient en peine,
  Quand je m'assis au bord de la premiere arene:
  Et voyant le bâteau qui s'enfuyoit de moy,
  Parlant à Marion je chantay ce convoy.

Bâteau qui par les flots ma chere vie emportes,
  Des vents en ta faveur les haleines soient mortes,
  Et le Ban perilleux qui se trouve parmy
  Les eaux, ne t'envelope en son sable endormy:
  Que l'air, le vent, et l'eau favorisent ma dame,
  Et que nul flot bossu ne destourbe sa rame.

En guise d'un estang sans vague paresseux
  Aille le cours de Loire et son limon crasseux
  Pour ce jourd'huy se change en gravelle menuë,
  Pleine de meint ruby et meinte perle esleuë.

Que les bords soient semez de mille belles fleurs,
  Representant sur l'eau mille belles couleurs,
  Et le tropeau Nymphal des gentilles Naïades
  Alentour du vaisseau face mille gambades:
  Les unes balloyant des paumes de leurs mains
  Les flots devant la barque, et les autres leurs seins
  Descouvrent à fleur d'eau, et d'une main ouvriere
  Conduisent le bâteau du long de la riviere.

L'azuré Martinet puisse voler davant
  Avecques la Mouétte, et le Plongeon suivant
  Son malheureux destin pour le jourd'huy ne songe
  En sa belle Esperie, et dans l'eau ne se plonge:
  Et le Heron criard, qui la tempeste fuit,
  Haut pendu dedans l'air ne face point de bruit:
  Ains tout gentil oiseau qui va cherchant sa proye
  Par les flots poissonneux, bien-heureux te convoye,
  Pour seurement venir avecq' ta charge au port,
  Où Marion voirra, peut estre, sur le bord
  Un orme des longs bras d'une vigne enlassée,
  Et la voyant ainsi doucement embrassée,

Already the oars hauled the round bellied boat,
The filling sail humped its great folds,
Took my heart's pleasure, and left sorrow there.
Watching the boat fly from me
I sang my Marion this formal song.

Oh, Boat! who took my dear life through the waves;
May killed winds stop their blowing in your favor,
And perilous shoals that hide under the current
Not wrap you in sleeping sands. Let air, wind, water,
Favor my lady; no bulging wave unship your oar.
Let the Loire be a lazy, waveless pond,
The clay bed of its course become bright gravel
For one day, scattered with pearls and rubies.
Let its banks foster acres of bright flowers
To stare back from the water in their colors.
Then herds of delicate slender Naiades
Will make their gambols all about the vessel:
Some sweep the ripples flat before the barque
With the palms of their hands, and others decorate
Their breasts with water lilies, and then haul
The barge along the river with their working hands.
The Martin, made of lapis lazuli,
Can fly behind them; the sea mew; diver,
Following his sad fate, for this one day not think
Of his sweet Hesper, and not take the plunge.
The squalling heron, shunning storm, high gliding
In the air, not make his noise; and so all gentle
Birds, all those who browse within the fish-filled waters,
Graciously be your convoy, take your charge
To its sure coming into port, where Marion
May see the long arms of a clinging vine
Wrap an elm's trunk, and so remember me
Seeing a tree so sweetly garlanded,
And wish it were myself she found to embrace there.

De son pauvre Perrot se pourra souvenir,
Et voudra sur le bord embrassé le tenir.

On dit au temps passé, que quelques uns changerent
En riviere leur forme, et eux mesmes nagerent
Au flot qui de leur sang goutte à goutte sailloit,
Quand leur corps transformé en eau se distilloit.

Que ne puis-je muer ma ressemblance humaine
En la forme de l'eau qui ceste barque emmeine?
J'irois en murmurant sous le fond du vaisseau,
J'irois tout alentour, et mon amoureuse eau
Baiseroit or sa main, ore sa bouche franche,
La suivant jusqu'au port de la Chapelle blanche:
Puis laissant mon canal pour jouyr de mon vueil,
Par le trac de ses pas j'irois jusqu'à Bourgueil,
Et là dessous un pin, couché sur la verdure,
Je voudrois revestir ma premiere figure.

Se trouve point quelque herbe en ce rivage icy
Qui ait le goust si fort, qu'elle me puisse ainsi
Muer comme fut Glauque, en aquatique monstre,
Qui homme ne poisson, homme et poisson se monstre?
Je voudrois estre Glauque, et avoir dans mon sein
Les pommes qu'Ippomane eslançoit de sa main
Pour gaigner Atalante: afin de te surprendre,
Je les ru'rois sur l'eau, et te ferois apprendre
Que l'or n'a seulement sur la terre pouvoir,
Mais qu'il peult de sur l'eau les femmes decevoir.

Or cela ne peult estre, et ce qui se peult faire,
Je le veux achever afin de te complaire,
Je veux soigneusement ce coudrier arroser,
Et des chapeaux de fleurs sur ses fueilles poser:
Et avecq'un poinçon je veux de sur l'escorce
Engraver de ton nom les six lettres à force,
Afin que les passans en lisant Marion,
Facent honneur à l'arbre entaillé de ton nom.

Je veux faire un beau lict d'une verte jonchée
De Parvanche fueillue encontre-bas couchée,
De Thin qui fleure bon, et d'Aspic porte-epy,

They say in ancient times, some changed their forms
To rivers, and themselves would swim the water
They became, bursting from blood and tears,
Their rippling bodies gradually growing weaker.
Why should I not now cast my human seeming
For water's shape and motion; I would carry
Her boat, and chuckle at its strumming keel
And so exist around her. I would be water love
To kiss her hand, to kiss her drinking frankly
And be her wake to port at the white chapel.
Then, leaving my canal to take my will,
I'd trace her footsteps right into Bourgueil
And there, couched on the grass below a pine
I might take on my human form again.

Is there no plant growing along this bank
That has a flavor strong enough to induce
A change like Glaucus's into a mer-creature
Who, neither fish nor man, seemed to be both?
I would be Glaucus, and I would have with me
The apples Hippomenes tossed Atalanta
To win the race and win her: so to gain you
I'd float my apples on the water, make you learn
Gold's power is not confined to ground only
But that it can betray a woman even on water.

Or if that could not be, I want to do
Whatever I might manage to charm you;
I'll bring water carefully to the hazel tree
And hang garlands of flowers on its leaves;
And with my knife I'll dig into its bark
Deeply, the six letters of your name
And passersby, when they read MARION
Will give honor to the tree carved with your name.

I'll make a soft bed of woven greenery,
Of the low creeping leafy periwinkle,
Thyme the sweet flowering, clustered lavender;
Sweet pennyroyal, torn from its earthy weave;
The water lily to encourage coolness,
Evergreen; and the stream side's living rushes.

D'odorant Poliot contre terre tapy,
De Neufard tousjours verd, qui la froideur incite,
Et de Jonc qui les bords des rivieres habite.

Je veux jusques au coude avoir l'herbe, et je veux
De roses et de liz couronner mes cheveux.
Je veux qu'on me défonce une pipe Angevine,
Et en me souvenant de ma toute divine,
De toy mon doux soucy, espuiser jusqu'au fond
Mille fois ce jourd'huy mon gobelet profond,
Et ne partir d'icy jusqu'à tant qu'à la lie
De ce bon vin d'Anjou la liqueur soit faillie.

Melchior Champenois, et Guillaume Manceau,
L'un d'un petit rebec, l'autre d'un chalumeau,
Me chanteront comment j'euz l'ame despourveuë
De sens et de raison si tost que je t'euz veuë:
Puis chanteront comment pour flechir ta rigueur
Je t'appellay ma vie, et te nommay mon cœur,
Mon œil, mon sang, mon tout: mais ta haute pensée
N'a voulu regarder chose tant abaissée,
Ains en me desdaignant, tu aimas autre part
Un, qui son amitié chichement te depart.
Voila comme il te prend pour mespriser ma peine,
Et le rustique son de mon tuyau d'aveine.

*   *   *

Puis ils diront comment les garçons du village
Disent que ta beauté tire desja sur l'âge,
Et qu'au matin le coq dés la poincte du jour
N'oyra plus à ton huis ceux qui te font l'amour.
« Bien fol est qui se fie en sa belle jeunesse,
« Qui si tost se derobe, et si tost nous delaisse.
« La rose à la parfin devient un gratecu,
« Et tout, avecq' le temps, par le temps est vaincu.

Quel passetemps prens-tu d'habiter la valée
De Bourgueil, où jamais la Muse n'est allée?
Quitte moy ton Anjou, et vien en Vandomois:
Là s'eslevent au ciel le sommet de noz bois,

I want to have grass elbow long. I want
My hair wreathed with the rose and lily.
I want someone to dig me up a jug
Of wine of Anjou, drain it a thousand times
Into my deep cup, minding the godliness
You've wished upon me, my sweet trouble. Let him not leave
Until the last drop of the liquor clouds with dregs.
Melchior, from Champagne, with his recorder,
And Bill the Mainer, blowing on his pipe,
Can sing to me how my soul is devoid
Of sense and reason since I first saw you.
Then they will sing how, to bend your resistance,
I called you my life, gave you my heart's own name,
My eye, my blood, my all; but that your high concern
Had no desire to look on so low a thing
And that, disdaining me, you loved another man
Whose love was doled out only stingily:
So this is your reward for having scorned my pain,
The country music of my oat straw pipe.

Then they will sing how the kids in the town
Say that your beauty is already aging
And that the morning cock, waking at daybreak,
Will not see lovers sneak out of your house:
Only a fool puts trust in youthful beauty.
It gives way so soon: so soon abandons us.
The sweet dog rose becomes a wrinkled haw
And all, in time, is beaten down by time.

Leave your Anjou, and come live in Vendôme
Where our trees' peaks hold the sky up. Thousands of groves,
Thousands of level plains are there; there rustle
The waters of a hundred thousand springs.
There echo skirts and rebounds from the rocks
Speaking my poems: can talk only of love.

Là sont mille taillis et mille belles plaines,
Là gargouillent les eaux de cent mille fontaines,
Là sont mille rochers, où Echon alentour
En resonnant mes vers ne parle que d'Amour.

Ou bien si tu ne veux, il me plaist de me rendre
Angevin pour te voir, et ton langage apprendre:
Et pour mieux te fléchir, les hauts vers que j'avois
En ma langue traduit du Pindare Gregeois,
Humble je veux redire en un chant plus facile
Sur le doux chalumeau du pasteur de Sicile.

Là parmy tes sablons Angevin devenu,
Je veux vivre sans nom comme un pauvre incognu,
Et dés l'aube du jour avecq' toy mener paistre
Aupres du port Guiet nostre tropeau champestre:
Puis sur le chaut du jour je veux en ton giron
Me coucher sous un chesne, où l'herbe à l'environ
Un beau lict nous fera de mainte fleur diverse,
Pour nous coucher tous deux sous l'ombre à la renverse:
Puis au Soleil penchant nous conduirons noz bœufs
Boire le hault sommet des ruisselets herbeux,
Et les reconduirons au son de la musette,
Puis nous endormirons de sur l'herbe molette.

Là sans ambition de plus grans biens avoir,
Contenté seulement de t'aimer et te voir,
Je passerois mon âge, et sur ma sepulture
Les Angevins mettroient ceste breve escriture.

Celuy qui gist icy, touché de l'aiguillon
Qu'amour nous laisse au cœur, garda comme Apollon
Les tropeaux de sa dame, et en ceste prairie
Mourut en bien aimant une belle Marie,
Et elle apres sa mort mourut aussi d'ennuy,
Et sous ce verd tombeau repose avecques luy.

A peine avois-je dit, quand Thoinet se dépâme,
Et à soy revenu alloit apres sa dame:
Mais je le retiray le menant d'autre part
Pour chercher à loger, car il estoit bien tard.

Or if it pleases you, I'll go to live
In Anjou, see you there, and learn your language;
And, to persuade you more efficiently,
The highflown poems I put into French
From Pindar's Greek, I'll humble down and sweeten
Into a simpler song, learned from the reed
Of the Sicilian shepherd, Theocritus.
Lost in your fine sands, I'll become Angevin.

I want to live without a name, and poor,
Near Port-Guyet, driving the cows to pasture
In the dawn with you; with you spend all my days
In meadows. In noon's heat I want to find
Your lap to sleep in under oak. Or I will make
Grass and the numerous flowers into a bed
We'll rest together in until the shadows shift.
Then we will lead our cows into the sunset
To drink the weedy surfaces of streams;
And lead them home accompanied by bagpipes.
And then we'll sleep again in the soft grasses.
I'd live my life out in complete contentment,
Desiring no more rare or wonderful,
For I would love and see you. And on my grave
The other Angevins could put this small inscription:

Here lies one in whose heart Love left its sting.
He kept, as Apollo did, his woman's herds, and died
In pasture, still in love with Mary.
She died shortly thereafter, of distress,
And sleeps here with him under this green hill.

Nous avions ja passé la sablonneuse rive,
Et le flot qui bruyant contre le pont arrive,
Et ja dessus le pont nous estions parvenus,
Et nous apparoissoit le tombeau de Turnus,
Quand le pasteur Janot tout gaillard nous emmeine
Dedans son toict couvert de javelles d'aveine.

I'd barely spoken. Thoinet came out of his faint
And at his coming-to, took off after his woman.
I dragged him back and forced him to go elsewhere
To find a place to sleep. It had become quite late.
We had already passed the sandy beach
And come to where the current splashes against the bridge;
Then we arrived at the bridge itself
And saw the tomb of Turnus, and his town,
Where Jack the Shepherd welcomed us heartily
Under his roof, thatched with the straw of oats.

37. RESPONSE AUX INJURES & CALOMNIES DE JE NE SCAY QUELS PREDICANS & MINISTRES DE GENEVE

Tu te plains d'autre part que ma vie est lascive,
En delices, en jeux, en vices excessive,
Tu mens mechantement: si tu m'avois suivi
Deux moys, tu sçaurois bien en quel estat je vy:
Or je veux que ma vie en escrit aparoisse:
Afin que pour menteur un chacun te cognoisse.

M'esveillant au matin, davant que faire rien,
J'invoque l'Eternel, le pere de tout bien,
Le priant humblement de me donner sa grace,
Et que le jour naissant sans l'offenser se passe,
Qu'il chasse toute secte & tout erreur de moy,
Qu'il me vueille garder en ma premiere foy,
Sans entreprendre rien qui blesse ma province,
Treshumble observateur des loys & de mon Prince.

Apres je sors du lict, & quant je suis vestu
Je me renge à l'estude, & aprens la vertu,
Comparant & lisant, suyvant ma Destinée,
Qui s'est des mon enfance aux Muses enclinée:
Quatre ou cinq heures seul je m'areste enfermé,
Puis sentant mon esprit de trop lire assommé
J'abandonne le livre, & m'en vois à l'Eglise:
Au retour pour plaisir une heure je devise,
De là je viens disner, faisant sobre repas,
Puis je rends grace à Dieu: au reste je m'esbas:

Car si l'apresdinée est plaisante & sereine,
Je m'en vais promener tantost parmy la plaine,
Tantost en un village, & tantost en un boys,
Et tantost par les lieux solitaires & coys,
J'ayme fort les jardins qui sentent le sauvage,
J'ayme le flot de l'eau qui gazoille au rivage.

Elsewhere, you complain that my life is lecherous
In pleasures, games, and outrageous vices.
That is a lie. If you had followed me two months
You would know the nature of my life.
I want my life put down in writing
So that your lies will appear plainly.

When I rise in the morning, before I do
Anything else, I ask the eternal father of all good
To give me grace. And I pray humbly
That this dawning day may pass
Without my offending Him; that He drive
Error and religious faction from me,
Guard me in my first faith
Without imposing injury to my country,
The humble servant of my prince, and of the law.

After rising, I dress, put myself to the study of proper action,
Write and read, as it was intended, ever since my boyhood,
That I follow my inclination toward these exercises.

I keep closeted, by myself, four or five hours.
Then, because my mind is heavy after too much reading,
I leave books and go out to church.
Then I converse for an hour or so, for pleasure,
Have my dinner—a modest enough meal—
Thank God for it; and then I take some exercise.
If the afternoon is calm and clear
I may go walking in the fields, or into town.
I may take to the woods
Through quiet, empty places.

Là devisant sur l'herbe aveq' un mien amy
Je me suis par les fleurs bien souvent endormy
A l'ombrage d'un saule, ou lisant dans un livre
J'ay cherché le moyen de me faire revivre,
Tout pur d'ambition & des soucis cuisans,
Miserables bourreaux d'un tas de mesdisans
Qui font (comme ravis) les prophettes en France,
Pipant les grands Seigneurs d'une belle apparence.

Mais quand le ciel est triste & tout noir d'espesseur,
Et qui ne fait aux champs ny plaisant ny bien seur,
Je cherche compagnie, ou je joüe à la prime,
Je voltige, ou je saute, ou je lutte, ou j'escrime,
Je di le mot pour rire, & à la verité
Je ne loge chés moy trop de severité.

J'ayme à faire l'amour, j'ayme à parler aux femmes,
A mettre par escrit mes amoureuses flames,
J'ayme le bal, la dance, & les masques aussi,
La musicque & le luth, ennemis du souci.

Puis quand la nuit brunette a rangé les estoilles
Encourtinant le ciel & la terre de voilles,
Sans soucy je me couche, & là levant les yeux,
Et la bouche & le cueur vers la voute des cieux,
Je fais mon oraison, priant la bonté haute
De vouloir pardonner doucement à ma faute.

Au reste je ne suis ni mutin ny meschant,
Qui fais croire ma loy par le glaive tranchant.
Voila comme je vy: si ta vie est meilleure,
Je n'en suis envieux: & soit à la bonne heure!

I love gardens that retain some wildness;
The way water whispers against earth at the stream's bank;
I may talk there, on the grass, with a friend,
And sometimes fall asleep in the flowers
In willow shadow. Or I read awhile,
Looking for some way to refresh myself,
Innocent of ambition, and free from what troubles torture
The miserable heap of ill speakers
Who pretend themselves France's inspired prophets,
And warble the good looks of the well-off.

If the sky is threatening or overcast
And the weather neither pleasant nor predictable
I seek out company; or I play poker;
I ride, jump, wrestle, fence,
Tell jokes. As a matter of fact
In general, I don't keep much severity in the house.
I enjoy making love. I love talking with women,
Putting the fires of my affections into writing;
I love dancing, and plays, music and the lute,
Sadness' enemies.

            Then, when the night has ranked its stars
And shrouds the earth and sky with dark veils,
I go to bed without worrying, and put
My prayers, heart, eye, and mouth, to the sky's vault,
Praying to the great good gently to pardon my faults.

And so, I am neither wicked, nor the mutinous sort
Who makes his law believed by armed force.
And this is how I live. If your life is better
Good luck to you. I don't envy you.

38. DISCOURS AMOUREUX DE GENEVRE

Genevre, je te prie, escoute ce discours
  Qui commence & finit nos premieres amours:
  Souvent le souvenir de la chose passée,
  Quand on le renouvelle, est doux à la pensée.

Sur le fin de Juillet que le chaut violent
  Rendoit de toutes pars le ciel estincelent,
  Un soir, à mon malheur, je me baignoy dans Seine,
  Où je te vy danser sur la rive prochaine,
  Foulant du pied le sable, & remplissant d'amour
  Et de ta douce voix tous les bords d'alentour.

Tout nud je me vins mettre entre ta compagnie,
  Où dansant je brulay d'une ardeur infinie,
  Voyant soubs la clarté brunette du croissant
  Ton oeil brun, à l'envy de l'autre apparoissant.

Là je baisay ta main pour premiere acointance,
  Autrement de ton nom je n'avois cognoissance:
  Puis d'un agile bond je m'eslançay dans l'eau,
  Pensant qu'elle esteindroit mon premier feu nouveau.
  Il advint autrement, car au milieu des ondes
  Je me senty lié de tes deux tresses blondes,
  Et le feu de tes yeux qui les eaux penetra
  Maugré la froide humeur dedans mon cœur entra.
  Dès le premier assaut je perdy l'asseurance:
  Je m'en allay coucher sans aucune esperence
  De jamais te revoir pour te donner ma foy,
  Comme ne cognoissant ny ta maison ny toy:
  Je ne te cognoissois pour la belle Genevre,
  Qui depuis me brusla d'une amoureuse fièvre:
  Aussi de ton costé tu ne me cognoissois
  Pour Ronsard ornement du langage François.

Sometimes it happens that the memory
Of past things, brought forward again,
Is pleasant to the thinking. Genevre, listen.
I will put here the start and finish of our earliest loving.

The entire sky sparkled with the violent heat
Of the end of July. To my misfortune
I swam in the Seine river in the evening,
And saw you dancing on the opposite bank,
Foot-battering the sand; your clear voice
Strode on the water's edge, and made love fill the river.

Completely naked, I plunged into your crowd,
Danced with you, burning with huge intentions,
But saw, under its clean dark crescent brow,
Your dark eye looked for the coming of a different man.

Well, so I kissed your hand to make acquaintance,
Knowing no more about you than your name;
And cast myself into the river again,
Thinking to quench the first spark of this fire.
It happened otherwise. At midstream
I felt myself tangled in two blonde strands,
And the fire of your eyes searching through the water
Entered my own, still burning, in the chill river.

I lost my confidence after the first attack,
Went to bed hopeless the chance would come
To see you and pledge my faith. I knew
Neither your house, nor you.
I did not know you for that Genevre, fevered
With an affection that burned for me already.

For your part, you did not know Ronsard,
The ornament of the French language, had
Danced for you. . . .

39. LE CHAT
AU SEIGNEUR DE BELLEAU

Dieu est par tout, par tout se mesle Dieu,
    Commencement, la fin, & le millieu
    De ce qui vit, & dont l'Ame est enclose
    Par tout, & tient en vigueur toute chose
    Come nostre Ame infuse dans noz corps.

Ja des longtemps les membres seroient morts
    De ce grand Tout, si cette Ame divine
    Ne se mesloit par toute la Machine,
    Luy donnant vie & force & mouvement:
    Car de tout estre elle est commencement.

Des Elements & de cette Ame infuse
    Nous somes nez: le corps mortel, qui s'use
    Par trait de temps, des Elementz est fait:
    De Dieu vient l'ame, & come il est parfait
    L'ame est parfaite, intouchable, immortelle,
    Come venant d'une Essence eternelle:
    L'Ame n'a doncq commencement ni bout:
    Car la Partie ensuit toujours le Tout.

Par la vertu de cette ame meslée
    Tourne le Ciel à la voute estoillée,
    La Mer s'esgaye, & la Terre produit
    Par les saisons, herbes, fueilles, & fruit,
    Je dy la Terre, heureuse part du monde,
    Mere benigne, à gros tetins fœconde,
    Au large sein: De là tous animaux,
    Les emplumez, les escadrons des eaux:
    De là Belleau, ceux qui ont pour repaire
    Où le rocher ou le le bois solitaire
    Vivent & sont, & mesme les metaux,
    Les Diamans, rubis Orientaux,

for Jacquie Block and Ben Martinez

God is throughout. God mingles in all things,
The beginning, end, and center of all life.
All things enclose His soul, and are made vigorous
By it, in the way our souls infuse our bodies.

The limbs of this all-things would have been dead
Long since, did not His soul mingle throughout
And give the machine its life, its force and motion.
God's soul is the beginning of all things.

Now, we are born of elements, and of this
Infused soul: the mortal body, which time
Wears into, is made up of the elements.
Soul comes of God, and, since He is perfect
The soul is perfect, permanent, untouchable,
As it must be. It comes of eternal essence.
The soul, therefore, has neither start nor finish
Since the part always imitates the whole.

It is by virtue of this mingled soul
The sky turns in its vault of stars. The sea
Quickens. The earth brings out in season, grass,
Leaves, and fruit; Earth, the world's glad partner,
Kind mother, broad of breast, and nourishing.
From soul all beasts, feathered or water-troops,
Belleau; from it all hunters of lone woodlands
Or cave, take life, and are: the metals even,
Diamonds, and rubies from the Orient,

Perles, saphirs, ont de là leur essence,
Et par telle ame ilz ont force & puissance,
Qui plus qui moins, selon qu'ils en sont pleins:
Autant en est de nous pauvres humains.

Ne voy-tu pas que la sainte Judée
Sur toute terre est plus recommandée
Pour aparoistre en elle des espritz
Ravis de Dieu, de Prophetie espriz?

Les regions, l'air, & le corps y servent
Qui l'ame saine en un corps sain conservent,
Car d'autant plus que bien sain est le corps
L'ame se montre & reluist par dehors.

Or come on voit qu'entre les homes naissent
Miracles grandes, des Prophetes qui laissent
Un tesmoignage à la posterité
Qu'il ont vescu pleins de divinité,
Et come on voit naistre ici des Sybilles
Par les troupeaux des femmes inutiles:
Ainsi voit-on, prophetes de noz maux,
Et de noz biens, naistre des animaux,
Qui le futur par signes nous predisent,
Et les mortels enseignent & avisent.
Ainsi le veult ce grand Pere de tous
Qui de sa grace a tousjours soing de nous.

Il a donné en cette Terre large
Par sa bonté aux animaux la charge
De tel soucy, pour ne douter de rien,
Ayant chez nous qui nous dit mal & bien.

De là sortit l'escolle de l'Augure
Merquant l'oyseau, qui par son vol figure
De l'advenir le pront evenement
Ravy de Dieu: & Dieu jamais ne ment.

En noz maisons ce bon Dieu nous envoye
Le Coq, la Poule, & le Canard, & l'Oye,
Qui vont monstrant d'un signe non obscur,
Soit se baignant ou chantant, le futur.

Sapphires and pearls, take essence out of it.
Their force and power come out of this soul,
Which varies according to the amount contained.
And so it is also with us poor humans.

Don't you see how blessed Judea
Is better known throughout the whole world
By the appearance there of souls that God
Took over: souls seized with the spirit of prophecy.

The regions, air, and the body, all will serve him
Who keeps clear soul within a healthy body.
The clearer in health the body is maintained,
The soul exhibits itself, and it shines through.

So, we see miracles born among men:
Prophets who leave us witness, who have lived
Filled with divinity; and we find also
Sybils born among useless crowds of women.
In the same way, prophets of our mischance
Or of our good, are born among animals
And predict the future to us by their signs,
Teaching and warning mortals. So God wills,
The father of all things, who cares for us always.

So that we may not wonder about events
He has generously given to the world's animals
The charge of the prediction of both good and evil.
Therefore we have the school of Augury,
Study of birds, who make, in flying, patterns
That signal the events that are to come.
They are God-filled. God will not lie through them.

God sends into our houses these birds: the cock,
The hen, the duck, the goose; who give plain signs
Of the future, by their manner of swimming, singing.

Herbes & fleurs & les arbres qui croissent
    En noz jardins, Prophetes aparoissent:
    J'en ay l'exemple, & par moy je le scay,
    Entens l'histoire, & je te diray vray.

Je nourrissois à la mode ancienne
    Dedans ma court une Thessalienne,
    Qui autrefois pour ne vouloir aimer
    Vit ses cheveux en fueille transformer,
    Dont la verdure en son Printemps demeure.

Je cultivois cette plante à toute heure,
    Je l'arrosois, la cerclois, & bechois
    Matin & soir: ah! trompé, je pensois
    M'en faire au chef une belle couronne,
    Telle qu'un Prince, en recompense donne
    A son Poëte, alors qu'il a chanté
    Un œuvre grand dont il est contenté.

Un rien estoit que je l'avois touchée,
    Quand de sa place elle fut arrachée
    Par un Daimon: une mortelle main
    Ne fit le coup: le fait fut trop soudain:
    En retournant je vy la plante morte
    Qui languissoit contre terre, en la sorte
    Que j'ai langui depuis dedans un lict:
    Et me disoit, le Daimon qui me suit
    Me fait languir, come une fiebvre quarte
    Te doibt blesmir. En pleurant je m'escarte
    Loing de ce meurdre, & soudain repassant
    Je ne vy plus le tyge languissant,
    Esvanouÿ come on voit une nuë
    S'esvanoïr sous la pronte venuë
    Ou de l'Auton ou de Boré, qui est
    Balay de l'air, souz qui le beau temps naist,
    Le beau serain, quand la courbe figure
    Du Ciel d'azur aparoist toute pure.

Deux mois apres un cheval qui rua
    De coups de pié l'un de mes gens tua,
    Luy escrageant d'une playe cruelle
    Bien loin du test la gluante cervelle.

Grass, flowers and trees grow prophetlike in gardens.
I have proof of it from my own experience.
I put the truth of it here, for your hearing:

I nourished in my courtyard a Thessalian
Woman, bay tree, in the ancient fashion.
She willed she would not love, and saw her hair
Transformed into the green leaves of constant spring.

I cared for that plant constantly; watered
And weeded, cultivated its roots, morning
And evening: stupidly imagined I
Would make a fine wreath to put on my head
Such as a prince might give to reward his poet
Supposing that prince pleased with some major work.

I gave it only the smallest touch. A Demon
Ripped it out of its rooting. Mortal hands
Could not have made so sudden a disaster.
I saw the dead plant lying on the ground
As I lay afterward, ill, in my bed.

The tree had told me this: The Demon follows
And fells me, and malaria follows you
To take its toll.
                    Crying, I leaped away
From this murder; but passing immediately
Again, I saw the trunk lay there no longer:
Had vanished as a cloud vanishes, the sky
Swept with the air of north or southerly wind.
Fair weather is born under the clearing
Arch, which shows its serene shape, now, pure and blue.

Two months later a runaway horse killed
One of my people with his hooves, crushing
The wet brain out of his skull in a cruel wound.

Luy trespassant m'apeloit par mon nom,
Me regardoit: signe qui n'estoit bon,
Car je pensay qu'un malheureux esclandre
Debvoit bien tost dessus mon chef descendre
Come il a fait: onze mois sont passez
Que j'ay de mal tous les membres cassez.

Mais par sur tous l'animal domestique
    Du triste Chat, a l'esprit prophetique:
    Et faisoient bien ces grands Ægyptiens
    De l'honorer, & leurs Dieux qui de chiens
    Avoient la face & la bouche aboyante.

L'Ame du Ciel en tout corps tournoyante
    Les pousse, anime, & fait aux homes voir
    Par eux les maulx ausquels ilz doibvent choir.

Home ne vit qui tant haïsse au monde
    Les Chats que moy d'une haine profonde,
    Je hay leurs yeux, leur front & leur regard:
    Et les voyant je m'enfuy d'autrepart,
    Tremblant de nerfs, de veines, & de membre,
    Et jamais Chat n'entre dedans ma chambre,
    Abhorrant ceux qui ne sçauroient durer
    Sans voir un Chat aupres eux demeurer:
    Et toutefois cette hydeuse beste
    Se vint coucher tout aupres de ma teste
    Cherchant le mol d'un plumeux oreiller,
    Où je soulois à gauche sommeiller:
    Car voulontiers à gauche je sommeille
    Jusqu'au matin que le Coq me resveille.

Le Chat cria d'un miauleux effroy,
    Je m'esveillé come tout hors de moy,
    Et en sursaut mes serviteurs j'apelle,
    L'un allumoit une ardente chandelle,
    L'autre disoit qu'un bon signe c'estoit
    Quand un chat blanc son maistre reflatoit,
    L'autre disoit que le Chat solitaire
    Estoit la fin d'une longue misere:

Et lors fronçeant les plis de mon sourcy,
    Le larme à l'œil, je leur responds ainsy.

Dying, he called me by my name, stared at me:
A signal of no good. I saw misfortune
Would follow on my head; and so it did.
My limbs were racked with pain for eleven months.

But above all domestic animals
The dismal cat has the spirit of prophecy.
Egyptians did wisely to honor cats,
And make their gods dog-headed, with barking mouths.

The soul of heaven turns inside all bodies,
Impels and animates them, and through them
Lets men see the misfortunes they must fall to.

I hate cats with a hatred and terror
No other man in the world can equal.
I hate their eyes, their faces, their expressions.
When I see them I hurry somewhere else,
My nerves, my veins, and all my limbs shaking.
And cats may never come into my room.
I abhor those who don't know how to survive
Without seeing a cat camping beside them.
At any rate, this hideous animal
Came and lay down right up against my head,
Finding the softness of the feather pillow
Where I was sleeping on my left side;
For I prefer sleeping on my left side
Until the cock wakes me up in the morning.

The cat cried with a frightful mewl. I woke,
Startled almost out of myself; yelled for my servants.
One lit a candle for me; and one said
When a white cat caressed its master
It was a good sign; and one said a cat
Alone, signaled the end of a long sadness.

But worry gathered its strands into sure knowledge.
I gave this answer to them, deeply troubled:

Le Chat devin miaulant signifie
   Une facheuse & longue maladie,
   Et que long temps je gard'ray la maison,
   Come le Chat qui en toute saison
   De son seigneur le logis n'abandonne,
   Et soit Printemps, soit Esté, soit Autonne
   Et soit Hyver, soit de jour soit de nuit,
   Ferme s'arreste, & jamais ne s'enfuit,
   Faisant la ronde & la garde eternelle
   Come un soldat qui fait la sentinelle,
   Avecq le Chien, & l'Oye dont la voix
   Au Capitole annonçea les Gaulois.

Autant en est de la tarde Tortuë,
   Et du Limas qui plus tard se remuë,
   Porte-maisons, qui toujours sur le dos
   Ont leur palais, leur lit, & leur repos,
   Lequel leur est aussi bel edifice
   Qu'un grand chasteau basty par artifice.
   L'homme qui voit, songeant, ces animaux,
   Peut bien penser que longs seront ses maux:
   Mais s'il voyoit une Gruë, ou un Cygne,
   Ou le Pluvier, cela luy seroit signe
   De voyager, car tels oyseaux sont prontz,
   A tire d'æsle ilz reviennent & vont
   En terre, en l'air, sans arrester une heure.

Autant en est du Loup qui ne demeure
   En son bocage, & cherche à voyager:
   Aux maladifz il est bon à songer:
   Il leur promet que bien tost sans dommage
   Sains & guariz feront quelque voyage.

Dieu qui tout peut, aux animaux permet
   De dire vray, & l'home qui ne met
   Creance en eux est du tout frenetique:
   Car Dieu par tout en tous se communique.

Mais quoy? je porte aux forests des rameaux,
   En l'Ocean des poissons & des eaux,
   Quand d'un tel vers mon Euterpe te flate,
   Qui as traduit, Belleau, le grand Arate,

The cat's clairvoyant screaming signifies
An illness that will be long and distressing:
And that I will be housebound for a long time,
Like the cat, who day and night, whatever season,
Spring, summer, autumn, winter, keeps to the house
Of his master without budging; will not leave,
But makes his rounds, and is a constant sentry,
A soldier on guard duty like a dog,
Or like the goose whose noise announced the Gauls.

In the same way turtles (slower still,
The snails), house-carriers, who have on their backs
Their palace, bed and rest—their edifice
Lovely as castles made by artifice:
The dreamer who looks on these animals
Should know the long duration of his misfortunes.
But if he dreams of crane, or swan, or plover,
Those are the signs of traveling; for such birds
Are quick of wing, pass between earth and sky
Without allowing even an hour to lapse.

It is a good thing for the sick man to dream of the wolf
Who roams in hunting outside of his thicket:
It promises that soon, healed, he will travel.

God is all powerful. He permits beasts
To speak the truth. The man who will not put
Credence in them, is frantic: because God
Communicates to all by means of all.

Les signes vrais des animaux certains,
Que Dieu concede aux ignorans humains
En leurs maisons, & qui n'ont cognoissance
Du cours du ciel ny de son influence
Enfans de terre: ainsy il plaist à Dieu,
Qui ses bontez eslargist en tout lieu,
Et pour aimer sa pauvre creature
A souz nos pieds soumis toute nature
Des animaux, d'autant que l'home est fait
Des animaux l'animal plus parfait.

But I am bringing branches to the woods,
Water and fish to ocean, so to flatter
Aratos's translator, Belleau. You know
The true signs of the various animals
That God has pleased to grant to stupid humans
To keep inside their houses, since they are ignorant
Of the sky's roads, and of its influence
On the world's children. So it pleased the Lord
Who spreads His bounties throughout all the world;
And out of love for His poor creature, placed
The nature of all animals below
Our feet; because of man He made most perfect
Animal, among all the animals.

40. LA SALADE
A AMA. JAMYN

Lave ta main blanche, gaillarde & nette,
  Suy mes talons, aporte une serviette,
  Allon cueillir la salade, & faison
  Part à noz ans des fruitz de la saison.
  D'un vague pas, d'une veuë escartée,
  Deçà delà jettée & rejettée,
  Or' sur la rive, ores sur un fossé,
  Or' sur un champ en paresse laissé
  Du laboureur, qui de luy-mesme aporte
  Sans cultiver herbes de toute sorte,
  Je m'en iray solitaire à l'escart.

Tu t'en iras, Jamyn, d'une autre part
  Chercher songneux, la boursette toffuë,
  La pasquerette à la fueille menuë,
  La pimprenelle heureuse pour le sang,
  Et pour la ratte, & pour le mal de flanc,
  Et je cueill'ray, compagne de la mousse,
  La responsette à la racine douce,
  Et le bouton de nouveaux groiseliers
  Qui le Printemps annoncent les premiers.

Puis en lysant l'ingenieux Ovide
  En ces beaux vers où d'Amour il est guide,
  Regangnerons le logis pas à pas:
  Là recoursant jusqu'au coude nos bras,
  Nous laverons nos herbes à main pleine
  Au cours sacré de ma belle fonteine,
  La blanchirons de sel en meinte part,
  L'arrouserons de vinaigre rosart,
  L'engresserons de l'huille de Provence:
  L'huille qui vient aux oliviers de France
  Rompt l'estomac, & ne vaut du tout rien.

for Virginia Savage

Wash your white hand. Let it be clean and supple.
Follow my heels, and bring a napkin with you,
And we will gather greens, go out to take
Our years' share of the season's fruitfulness.

I'll go alone, to out of the way corners,
Wandering without a planned itinerary,
Tossed and rebounding from streamside to gutter,
In fields left fallow by the plowman,
That, left untilled, bear on their own all sorts
Of greens. Jamyn, you must look carefully
In other places, for lamb's lettuce; marguerites
Whose leaves are still slender; salad burnet
The blood stauncher, good for the spleen and for
Aches in the side. I'll gather rampion,
Mosses' companion, sweet of root; and buds
From the new gooseberry bushes, Spring's first announcers.

Then, reading Ovid's intelligent verses,
The Art of Love, to which he is the guide,
We'll come back into the house in lockstep.
There, stripping our arms back up to the elbows,
We'll wash fistfulls of greens in holy water
Out of my lovely spring; then with fine salt
We'll whiten it, damp it with rosé vinegar,
And make it rich with Provence olive oil.
(The oil that comes from our French walnuts is
Hard on the stomach, and completely useless.)

Voilà, Jamyn, voilà mon souv'rain bien,
  En attendant que de mes veines parte
  Cette execrable horrible fiebvre quarte
  Qui me consomme & le corps & le cœur
  Et me fait vivre en extreme langueur.

Tu me diras que la fiebvre m'abuze,
  Que je suis fol, ma salade & ma Muse:
  Tu diras vray: je le veux estre aussy,
  Telle fureur me guarist mon soucy.
  Tu me diras que la vie est meilleure
  Des importuns, qui vivent à toute heure
  Aupres des Grandz en credit, & bonheur,
  Enorgueilliz de pompes & d'honneur:
  Je le sçay bien, mais je ne le veuz faire,
  Car telle vie à la mienne est contraire.

Il faut mentir, flater, & courtizer,
  Rire sans ris, sa face deguiser
  Au front d'autruy, & je ne le veux faire,
  Car telle vie à la mienne est contraire.
  Je suis pour suivre à la trace une Court,
  Trop maladif, trop paresseux, & sourd,
  Et trop creintif: au reste je demande
  Un doux repos, & ne veux plus qu'on pende
  Comme un pongnard, les soucis sur mon front.

En peu de temps les Courtizans s'en vont
  En chef grison, ou meurent sur un coffre.
  Dieu pour salaire un tel present leur offre
  D'avoir gasté leur gentil naturel
  D'ambition & de bien temporel,
  Un bien mondain, qui s'enfuit à la trace,
  Dont ne jouïst l'acquereur, ny sa race:
  Ou bien, Jamin, ilz n'auront point d'enfans,
  Ou ilz seront en la fleur de leurs ans
  Disgratiez par Fortune ou par vice,
  Ou ceux qu'ilz ont retrompez d'artifice
  Les apastant par subtilles raisons,
  Feront au Ciel voller leurs oraisons:

Jamyn, to do this will be healthful for me:
The sovereign remedy to make my veins give up
The ghastly fevers of malaria
That wither both my body and my heart
And cloud my living with such dreadful torpor.

You'll say my fever has gone to my head,
Presumes upon my salad and my muse;
And that will be true. I wish it to be, as well.
Some madness might at least cure my depression.
And will you say the boring courtier lives
A better life, who lives next to the great
In credit and well-being, puffed with pride,
Parades and honors? Well, I know it's true;
But I don't want to lead that kind of life.
It is against my natural way of living.

Courtiers must lie, flatter, and fawn,
Laugh without humor, hide their real expressions
In front of others: which I prefer not to do
Since it is against my natural way of living.
I am too ill, too lazy, too deaf and nervous
To follow the court's road; I demand instead
Just quiet rest. I don't need them to hang
Their worries and troubles over me like daggers.

Courtiers will shortly find their hair gone gray
And then die on the dole. God makes their salary
Their having spoiled their natural nobleness
With their ambition; their eternal good
With worldly welfare, that diaphanous prey
That won't please its acquirer, nor his heirs.
And, Jamyn, either they will have no offspring
Or they will die disgraced by vice or fortune
When they are at the flower of their years.
Or those they have betrayed by their conniving
Will pay them back through careful tactics, make
Them send up flocks of their clapping players to heaven.

Dieu s'en courrouce, & veux qu'un pot de terre
Soit foudroyé, sans qu'il face la guerre
Contre le Ciel, & serve qu'en tout lieu
L'Ambition est desplaisante à Dieu,
Et la faveur qui n'est que vaine bouë,
Dont le destin en nous moquant se jouë:
D'où la Fortune aux retours inconstans
A la parfin les tombe malcontens,
Montrant à tous par leur cheute soudaine
Que c'est du vent que la farce mondaine,
Et que l'home est tresmal'heureux qui vit
En court estrange, & meurt loing de son lit.

Loing de moy soit la faveur & la pompe,
Qui d'aparence, en se fardant, nous trompe,
Ains qui nous lime & nous ronge au dedans
D'ambition & de soucis mordans.
L'ambition, les soucis & l'envie,
Et tout cela qui meurdrist nostre vie,
Semblent des Dieux à tel hommes, qui n'ont
Ny foy au cœur, ný honte sur le front:
Telz hommes sont colosses inutilles,
Beaux par dehors, dedans pleins de chevilles,
Barres & clous qui serrent ces grandz corps:
En les voyant dorez par le dehors,
Un Jupiter, Appollon, ou Neptune,
Chacun revere & doute leur fortune:
Et toutefois tel ouvrage trompeur,
Par sa haulteur ne fait seulement peur
Qu'aux idiotz: mais l'homme qui est sage
Passant par là ne fait cas de l'ouvrage:
Ains en esprit il desdaigne ces Dieux,
Portraits de plastre, & luy fachent les yeux,
Subjets aux vents, au froid & à la poudre.
Le pauvre sot qui voit rougir la foudre
A longs rayons dedans leur dextre main,
Ou le trident à trois pointes d'airain,
Craint & pallist devant si grand Colosse,
Qui n'a vertu que l'aparence grosse,
Lourde, pesante, & qui ne peut en rien
Aux regardans faire ny mal ny bien,
Sinon aux fatz, où la sottize abonde,
Qui à credit craignent le rien du Monde.

This makes God's anger. He wills that the clay vessel
Be struck down, rather than it make war on heaven,
And so lets it be proof that ambition
Displeases God; and all favor is trash
Whose destiny tricks men, and teases with.
So fortune twists, and waywardly sees to it
That they fall at the end, in discontent.
Fortune shows all, by these sudden disasters,
That the world's stuffing is made out of wind.
And so it is an unhappy man who lives
In a strange court, and dies far from his bed.

The look of favor, and of ceremony,
Tricks us, since it appears decorative;
While it wears down and gnaws at us inside
With acids of pressure and ambition.
Ambition, desire, worry, all these things
Murder our lives, and seem like gods to men
Faithless at heart, who have no sense of shame.
Such men are like useless, sculpted colossuses,
Whose shining skins are stuffed with armatures

And bolts and nails that hold their bodies together.
A gilded Jupiter, Neptune, or Apollo
May impress some who can revere such fortunes;
But only idiots could be struck dumb
By the mass and mimicry of these pretentious works.
Real wisdom will make nothing of the image
And know these plaster gods visual irritants,
The wind's subjects, collectors of dust and cold.
A poor fool, when he sees the lightning glow
In Jupiter's right hand, or the brass points
Of Neptune's trident; goes pale with fright
Before these colossal statues, even though
Their only power lies in their apparent largeness,
Their bulk and weight. They'll do neither good nor harm
To the onlookers (unless they are conceited
Or stupid enough to trust in the empty world.)

Les pauvres sotz dignes de tous mechefz
  Ne sçavent pas que c'est un jeu d'eschetz
  Que nostre courte & miserable vie,
  Et qu'aussy tost que la Mort l'a ravie
  Dedans le sac somes mis à la fois
  Tous pesle mesle, & Laboureurs & Rois,
  Valetz, Seigneurs en mesme sepulture.
  Telle est la loy de la bonne Nature,
  Et de la Terre, en son ventre qui prend
  De fosse egalle & le Pauvre & le Grand,
  Et montre bien que la gloire mondaine,
  Et la grandeur est une chose vaine.

Ah! que me plaist ce vers Virgilian
  Où le vieillard pere Corytian
  Avecq' sa marre en travaillant cultive
  A tour de bras sa terre non oysive
  Et vers le soir sans achepter si cher
  Vin en taverne, ou chair chez le boucher,
  Alloit chargeant sa table de viandes,
  Qui luy sembloient plus douces & friandes
  Avecq la faim, que celles des Seigneurs
  Pleines de pompe & de fardez honneurs,
  Qui, desdaigneux, de cent viandes changent
  Sans aucun goust: car sans goust ilz les mangent.

These men are fools, and deserve any mischance.
They cannot see this for a game of chess;
Nor that our short and miserable life
Is ravaged quick enough by death, the mixer.
We will be cast pell mell into that bag,
Workers and kings together. Lords and their valets
Will both be thrown together into the same tombs.
This is the law of nature, and of the earth,
Who keeps ditched in her belly equal spaces
For simple and great men, and thereby shows us
That worldly glory and grandeur are vain things.

I'm always touched so pleasantly by Vergil's verses
Where the old man, with his short-handled hoe,
Is working, cultivating his labored land.
When evening comes, he turns down the expense
Of wine drunk in a tavern, and butcher's flesh;
And serves his own table with his kind of food
That seems to him sweeter and tastier
Because he is hungry, than that eaten by lords,
Who prance parading in, made fat with compliments,
And then disdainfully try a hundred dishes
And taste none; because they eat them without tasting.

Of these two men, which is the happier:
Important Crassus, with his fertile fields
Of shields, who, lacking Pompey's Roman triumph,
Went off to try the Parthian sword the hard way;
Or this old man who cultivates his field,
Lives in his garden, and never heard of Rome?

Hesiod said that if we only knew
How to eat asphodel, and how to grow it,
We would be happy men. The Mean surpasses
The All. Now, by the Mean he meant that life
Without decoration led by laborers
Who, by their arm's work, make their living healthy.
And by the All, he meant king's delicacies.

Lequel des deux estoit le plus heureux,
Ou ce grand Crasse en escus plantureux,
Qui pour n'avoir les honneurs de Pompée
Alla sentir la Parthienne espée,
Ou ce vieillard qui son champ cultivoit
Et sans voir Rome en son jardin vivoit?

Si nous sçavions, ce disoit Hesiode,
    Combien nous sert l'asphodelle, & la mode
De l'acoutrer, heureux l'home seroit,
Et la Moitié le Tout surpasseroit:
Par la Moitié il entendoit la vie
Sans aucun fard des laboureurs suivie,
Qui vivent sains du labeur de leurs doigtz,
Et par le Tout les delices des Rois.
La Nature est, ce dit le bon Horace,
De peu contente, & nostre humaine race
Ne quiert beaucoup: mais nous la corrompons
Et par le trop Nature nous trompons.

C'est trop presché: donne moy ma salade:
    El' ne vaut rien (dis-tu) pour un malade!

Hé! quoy, Jamyn, tu fais le Medecin!
    Laisse moy vivre au moins jusqu'à la fin
Tout à mon aise, & ne sois triste Augure
Soit à ma vie ou à ma mort future,
Car tu ne peux, ny moy, pour tout secours
Faire plus longs ou plus petis mes jours:
Il faut charger la barque Stygieuse:
La barque, c'est la Biere sommeilleuse,
Faite en bateau: le naistre est le trepas:
Sans naistre icy l'home ne mourroit pas:
Fol qui d'ailleurs autre bien se propose,
Naissance & mort est une mesme chose.

And Horace said that nature is content
With little; that the human race
Does not require much; that we corrupt it;
That Nature undermines us with her bounty.

I've said too long a grace. Pass me my salad.

You say that it will do no good for a sick man?
You're going to play the doctor now, Jamyn?
Let me just live until the end comes for me,
At my own ease. I don't need a grim prophet
To warn me that I'm going to live and die.
Whatever we do, neither you nor I
Can make my days run either longer or shorter.
The boat that floats toward death will be filled up.

(The boat that is the sleeper's catafalque
Made seaworthy)
                        The birth is in the dying.
Men would not die unless they were born to this.
Only a fool could hope some kinder ending.
Dying and being born are the same thing.

41. ODELETTE

Cependant que ce beau mois dure,
   Mignonne, allon sur la verdure,
   Ne laisson perdre en vain le temps:
   L'age glissant qui ne s'arreste,
   Meslant le poil de nostre teste,
   S'enfuit ainsy que le Printemps:

Doncq ce pendant que nostre vie,
   Et le temps d'aimer nous convie,
   Aimon, moissonnon noz desirs,
   Passon l'Amour de veine en veine,
   Incontinent la mort prochaine
   Viendra desrober noz plaisirs.

We must not let this sweet month
Vanish without purpose
Darling, but go among the grass.

Age glides and goes like spring
Time; mingles the hair of our heads.

We must be lovers. We must harvest
Desire, while our lives invite that;
Pass love from one vein to the next.

Death suddenly
Will come to tear our pleasures from us.

42.

Comme on voit sur la branche au mois de May la rose
En sa belle jeunesse, en sa premiere fleur
Rendre le ciel jaloux de sa vive couleur,
Quand l'Aube de ses pleurs au poinct du jour l'arrose:

La grace dans sa fueille, & l'amour se repose,
Embasmant les jardins et les arbres d'odeur:
Mais batue ou de pluye, ou d'excessive ardeur,
Languissante elle meurt fueille à fueille déclose:

Ainsi en ta premiere & jeune nouveauté,
Quand la terre & le ciel honoroient ta beauté,
La Parque t'a tuée, & cendre tu reposes.

Pour obseques reçoy mes larmes & mes pleurs,
Ce vase plein de laict, ce panier plein de fleurs,
Afin que vif, & mort, ton corps ne soit que roses.

Your body will be roses, living or dead.
As the rose cleaves to its stem, first blooming,
Young, making the sky alarmed with color,
Drenched with dawn,

Its petals give way gracefully to each other,
Bathing whole orchard gardens with its scent.

Rain thrashes, and the hot winds take
One petal, and another. And you

New still, are ashes suddenly?

I bring you my tears, this vase of milk,
This basket filled with flowers.

43.

Ce premier jour de may, Helene, je vous jure
  Par Castor, par Pollux, vos deux freres jumeaux,
  Par la vigne enlassee a l'entour des ormeaux,
  Par les prez, par les bois herissez de verdure,

Par le nouveau Printemps, fils aisné de Nature,
  Par le cristal qui roule au giron des ruisseaux,
  Par tous les rossignols, miracle des oiseaux,
  Que seule vous serez ma derniere aventure.

Vous seule me plaisez, j'ay par election
  Et non a la volee aimé vostre jeunesse:
  Aussi je prens en gré toute ma passion,

Je suis de ma fortune autheur, je le confesse:
  La vertu m'a conduit en telle affection.
  Si la vertu me trompe, adieu belle Maistresse.

May first. I make you this promise,
Helen, before witnesses: Castor and Pollux,
Your twin brothers; the vine gripping the elm;
The fields; the trees just prickling with small green;
Clear running water; miracles of birds:

You will be my last venture. I have loved your youth
By careful aim, not randomly. You alone please me.

I have made my passion subject to my will,
And am responsible for what will come of this.
Courage has led me into great affection.
If courage makes me foolish, I will go quietly.

44.

Ces longues nuicts d'hyver, où la Lune ocieuse
    Tourne si lentement son char tout à l'entour,
    Où le Coq si tardif nous annonce le jour,
    Où la nuit semble un an à l'ame soucieuse:

Je fusse mort d'ennuy sans ta forme douteuse,
    Qui vient par une feinte alleger mon amour,
    Et faisant toute nue entre mes bras sejour,
    Me pipe doucement d'une joye menteuse.

Vraye tu es farouche, et fiere en cruauté:
    De toy fausse on jouyst en toute privauté.
    Pres ton mort je m'endors, pres de luy je repose:

Rien ne m'est refusé. Le bon sommeil ainsi
    Abuse par le faux mon amoureux souci.
    S'abuser en amour n'est pas mauvaise chose.

Long winter nights. This sullen moon
Turns lazily its single rolling circle.
The cock crows day to us so late. So long
This sad night occupies my mind with boredom.

Even good sleep escapes me, fills itself
With falseness. Can it be wrong
To let love lead me into fantasy?

I sleep next to your double, and enjoy you
In this false privacy. Your pride,
Your cruel wildness, do not reach my invention.

Now come the tricks and lies, drawn together gently
Into your body—sham—but even so
Naked here beside me, and my arms around you.

45.

Quand vous serez bien vieille, au soir à la chandelle,
    Assise aupres du feu, devidant et filant,
    Direz chantant mes vers, en vous esmerveillant,
    Ronsard me celebroit du temps que j'estois belle.

Lors vous n'aurez servante oyant telle nouvelle,
    Desja sous le labeur à demy sommeillant,
    Qui au bruit de mon nom ne s'aille resveillant,
    Benissant vostre nom de louange immortelle.

Je seray sous la terre et fantôme sans os
    Par les ombreux myrteux je prendray mon repos:
    Vous serez au fouyer une vieille accroupie,

Regrettant mon amour et vostre fier desdain.
    Vivez, si m'en croyez, n'attendez à demain:
    Cueillez dés aujourdhuy les roses de la vie.

You will become old. You will learn to knit
And read by candlelight when you are sleepless
The poems here, that made you marvelous.
You were beautiful.

                   Already drowsy with firelight
And the tedious march of words, you catch
And start. The book makes blessings on you.
It is my name—Ronsard—against your fingers;
A name you have heard spoken with real sound.

I will be tangled in the roots of myrtle,
A boneless ghost, a shadow hovering
Below the skin of earth. You, crippled

With age, will find bare
Memory in your arms—my love, your proud refusal,
And the stripped stem from which the rose has fallen,
And its leaves; unless you take me, living, now.

46.

Mon ame mille fois m'a predit mon dommage:
　　Mais la sotte qu'elle est, apres l'avoir predit,
　　Maintenant s'en repent, maintenant s'en desdit,
　　Et voyant ma Maistresse elle aime d'avantage.

Si l'ame, si l'esprit qui sont de Dieu l'ouvrage,
　　Deviennent amoureux, à grand tort on mesdit
　　Du corps qui suit les Sens, non brutal comme on dit
　　S'il se trouve esblouy des raiz d'un beau visage.

Le corps ne languiroit d'un amoureux souci,
　　Si l'ame, si l'esprit ne le vouloient ainsi.
　　Mais du premier assaut l'ame est toute esperdue,

Conseillant, comme Royne, au corps d'en faire autant.
　　Ainsi le Citoyen trahy du combattant
　　Se rend aux ennemis, quand la ville est perdue.

I have recognized my downfall enough.
Love makes a fool of me, and recognition
Is followed always by repentance and denial,
And when I see you again, I fall, and love more firmly.

If the soul, which is God's work, becomes affectionate,
It is a lie to say of the body that it follows the senses
Brutally. The senses are staggered by beauty.

The body follows soul and the free will
Into attentive care, after the soul is struck
And lost. Good counsel tells the body, follow.

The surrounded city, its defenses breached,
Gives up its citizens to the besieger.

47.

Au milieu de la guerre, en un siecle sans foy,
    Entre mille procez, est-ce pas grand folie
    D'escrire de l'Amour? De manotes on lie
Des fols, qui ne sont pas si furieux que moy.

Grison & maladif r'entrer dessous la loy
    D'Amour, ô quelle erreur! Dieux, mercy je vous crie.
    Tu ne m'es plus Amour, tu m'es une Furie,
Qui me rends fol, enfant, & sans yeux comme toy:

Voir perdre mon pays, proye des adversaires,
    Voir en noz estendars les fleurs de liz contraires,
    Voir une Thebaïde, & faire l'amoureux.

Je m'en vais au Palais: adieu vieilles Sorcieres.
    Muses, je prens mon sac, je seray plus heureux
    En gaignant mes procez, qu'en suivant voz rivieres.

This is a faithless age. I am surrounded by war;
Am in the midst of court proceedings. Is it not great folly
To write about love now? Madmen less
Frantic than I, they put into cuffs.

Ill and white-headed I come under love's laws again.
Such a mistake! God, I must beg your mercy.
You are no love. You are a fury to me,
Make me resemble you, a mad, blind child.

To see my country lost, prey to the enemy.
The iris of our flags opposed
In fratricidal war: and play the lover!

I'll get back to the courtroom with my briefs.
Muses, you ancient witches, I will be happier
Winning my case, than following your rivers.

48.

Ma Dame, je me meurs abandonné d'espoir:
  La playe est jusqu'à l'oz: je ne suis celuy mesme
  Que j'estois l'autre jour, tant la douleur extrême,
  Forçant la patience, a dessus moy pouvoir.

Je ne puis ny toucher, gouster, n'ouyr ny voir:
  J'ay perdu tous mes sens, je suis une ombre blesme:
  Mon corps n'est qu'un tombeau. Malheureux est qui aime,
  Malheureux qui se laisse à l'Amour decevoir!

Devenez un Achille aux playes qu'avez faites,
  Un Telefe je suis, lequel s'en va perir:
  Monstrez moy par pitié voz puissances parfaites,

Et d'un remede prompt daignez moy secourir.
  Si vostre serviteur, cruelle, vous desfaites,
  Vous n'aurez le Laurier pour l'avoir fait mourir.

The wound is to the bone. I am no longer the man I was.
I see my death abandoned to despair.
Patience is cast off, with the power to move,
In extremis.

                 My senses shut, tongue, ears,
Eyes, fingers; all bandaged in shadow,
Stone: my body is my carved tomb.

This is a mortal wound made by your hand
Unless you bring your hand to touch it.

Show me your perfect pity and your power.
You will receive no glory for my death.
Let you heal me.

49.

Voyant par les soudars ma maison saccagee,
    Et mon païs couvert de Mars et de la mort,
    Pensant en ta beauté tu estois mon suport,
    Et soudain ma tristesse en joye estoit changee.

Resolu je disois, Fortune s'est vangee,
    Elle emporte mon bien et non mon reconfort,
    Hà, que je fus trompé! tu me fais plus de tort
    Que n'eust fait une armee en bataille rangee.

Les soudars m'ont pillé, tu as ravy mon cœur:
    Tu es plus grand voleur, j'en demande justice
    Aux Dieux qui n'oseroient chastier ta rigueur.

Tu saccages ma vie en te faisant service:
    Encores te mocquant tu braves ma langueur,
    Qui me fait plus de mal que ne fait ta malice.

I see my house ransacked by soldiers.
Death and war cover my country.
My sadness turns to joy. Your beauty
Has come over my thinking. You support me.

Time takes revenge, and my well-being,
Beyond comfort. Ha! I am set up
For ambush. I could be a batallion carefully assembled
Facing the wrong direction.

I am laid waste. My heart is torn
From me by the great thief, yourself,
The pillager. Scorched earth, my life in your service.

And now you taunt my disarray.
Your mocking does more damage than plain cruelty.

50.

Helas! voicy le jour que mon maistre on enterre:
   Muses, accompagnez son funeste convoy.
   Je voy son effigie, & au dessus je voy
   La Mort, qui de ses yeux la lumiere luy serre.

Voila comme Atropos les Majestez atterre
   Sans respect de jeunesse, ou d'empire, ou de foy.
   Charles qui fleurissoit nagueres un grand Roy,
   Est maintenant vestu d'une robbe de terre.

Hé! tu me fais languir par cruauté d'amour:
   Je suis ton Promethée, & tu es mon Vautour.
   La vengeance du Ciel n'oublira tes malices.

Un mal au mien pareil puisse un jour t'avenir,
   Quand tu voudras mourir, que mourir tu ne puisses.
   Si justes sont les Dieux, je t'en verray punir.

Today my master is set into the ground
And I must follow the sad procession, look
At his effigy, where death himself
Squats, and blocks his marble eyes with shadow.

My Charles is clothed with earth, felled,
No quarter given his greenness, faith, the strength
Of his empire: a king struck in full flower.

I have carried fire for you. And anguished
Now, I find your hooked beak in my heart.
Heaven will not forget this when your time to die
Comes, and death fails you, if there is justice.

Do you see how love and cruelty work in me
And make me wish revenge were possible?

51.

Je chantois ces Sonets, amoureux d'une Heleine,
   En ce funeste mois que mon Prince mourut:
   Son sceptre, tant fust grand, Charles ne secourut,
   Qu'il ne payast sa debte à la Nature humaine.

La Mort fut d'une part, & l'Amour qui me meine,
   Estoit de l'autre part, dont le traict me ferut,
   Et si bien la poison par les veines courut,
   Que j'oubliay mon maistre, attaint d'une autre peine.

Je senty dans le cœur deux diverses douleurs,
   La rigueur de ma Dame, & la tristesse enclose
   Du Roy, que j'adorois pour ses rares valeurs.

La vivante & le mort tout malheur me propose:
   L'une aime les regrets, & l'autre aime les pleurs:
   Car l'Amour & la Mort n'est qu'une mesme chose.

Love and death are close neighbors.
Weeping, the sense of loss—they are the company
Of my dead king, and you, living.

The king I loved as well, grief and desire
Are mingled in my veins like poison.

This is what humans come to. We have a debt to death.
And is it love leading us on to the same finish?

I have made poems of my love in the same month
Charles, my fine king, lay dying, Helen.

52. ELEGIE

Voicy le temps, Candé, qui joyeux nous convie
Par l'amour, par le vin, d'esbattre nostre vie:
L'an reprend sa jeunesse, & nous monstre comment
Il faut ainsi que luy, rajeunir doucement.
Ne vois-tu pas, Candé, ces jeunes Arondelles,
Ces Pigeons tremoussans & du bec & des ailes,
Se baiser goulument, & de nuict & de jour
Sur le haut d'une tour se soulasser d'amour?

Ne vois-tu pas comment ces Vignes enlassees
Tiennent de grands Ormeaux les branches embrassees?
Regarde ce bocage, & voy d'une autre part
Les bras longs & tortus du lhierre grimpart
En serpent se virer à l'entour de l'escorce
De ce chesne aux longs bras, & le baiser à force.

N'ois-tu le Rossignol, chantre Cecropien,
Qui se plaint toute nuict du forfait ancien
Du malheureux Theree, & d'une langue habile
Gringoter par les bois la mort de son Ityle?
Il reprend, il retient, il recoupe le son
Tantost haut, tantost bas, de sa longue chanson,
Apprise sans nul maistre, & d'une forte haleine
Raconte de sa sœur les larmes & la peine.

Ne vois-tu d'autre part les Nymphes dans ces prez
Esmaillez, peinturez, verdurez, diaprez,
D'un poulce delicat moissonner les fleurettes
Qui devoient estre proye aux gentilles avettes,
Lesquelles en volant de sillons en sillons,
De jardins en jardins avec les papillons,
A petits branles d'aile amassent mesnageres . . .

for Philip Herzbrun

Candé, this time invites us, joyous
With love and wine, to sport with life.
The year becomes young gracefully,
Shows us how to renew.

Candé, don't you see the young swallows;
The pigeons, beak- and wing-fluttering
In gluttonous kisses night and day; and how
They console themselves for love on their high tower?

And laced vines
Embrace the elm's heavy branches.
You see this grove. Now see the snaking
Long twists of the reaching, climbing ivy
Take to the turned bark of the long armed oak,
Force kisses on it.

Hear the Athenian singer, nightingale,
Who sings all night about the ancient forfeit
Of Tereus, whose son was served up to him. Her facile tongue
Takes, and recouples, sound in the woods now
In her love song. This song needed no teacher.
It is the sadness and the pain of Itys' mother, too,
Armed with her crying.

And you should see nymphs
In the leaved, painted, enameled, planished meadows,
Gathering flowers delicately,
That should be prey to gentle bees
Who fly along the furrows. Butterflies,
Garden to garden, their flat wings wag
Husbanding the transient scents of spring flowers . . .

53.

Si le grain de forment ne se pourrist en terre,
  Il ne sçauroit porter ny fueille, ny bon fruit:
  De la corruption la naissance se suit,
  Et comme deux anneaux l'un en l'autre s'enserre.

Le Chrestien endormy sous le tombeau de pierre
  Doit revestir son corps en despit de la nuit:
  Il doit suivre son Christ, qui la Mort a destruit,
  Premier victorieux d'une si forte guerre.

Il vit assis là-haut, trionfant de la Mort:
  Il a veincu Satan, les Enfers, & leur Fort,
  Et a fait que la Mort n'est plus rien qu'un passage,

Qui ne doit aux Chrestiens se monstrer odieux,
  Auquel Charle' est passé pour s'en-voler aux Cieux,
  Prenant pour luy le gain, nous laissant le dommage.

If the wheat grain did not rot in the ground
It would not know how to bear leaf or fruit.
Coming to birth grows out of corruption
And like two rings, one clasps the other.

The Christian sleeping in his tomb of stone
Must clothe his body again, and defy darkness.
And he must follow Christ, who destroyed death,
Who was the first victor in this battle.

He lives, seated on high, death's master,
Satan's, and Hell's, and all their stronghold's master:
He made of death no more than a brief passageway

The Christian should not fear.
Charles has passed through, and takes himself to heaven.
He is richer for it, and leaves all of us poorer.

54.

Vous estes deja vieille, & je le suis aussi.
   Joignon nostre vieillesse & l'accollon ensemble,
   Et faison d'un hyver qui de froidure tremble
   (Autant que nous pourrons) un printemps adouci.

Un homme n'est point vieil s'il ne le croit ainsi:
   Vieillard n'est qui ne veut: qui ne veut, il assemble
   Une nouvelle trame à sa vieille: & ressemble
   Un serpent rajeuni quand l'an retourne ici.

Ostez moy de ce fard l'impudente encrousture,
   On ne sçauroit tromper la loy de la nature,
   Ny derider un front condamné du miroir,

Ni durcir un tetin desja pendant & flasque.
   Le Temps de vostre face arrachera le masque,
   Et deviendray un Cygne en lieu d'un Corbeau noir.

You are already old; and I am old.
We should join our old ages and embrace each other.
We should make Spring where shivering Winter
Was, so far as we find that in our power.

We are not old unless we believe it.
One is not an old man against his will;
And, if he wills, he makes a new life string
Whip like a peeled snake into the new year.

Take off the disrespectful crust of paint.
You can not fiddle with the inevitable,
Nor patch the wrinkles the mirror condemns you to,
Nor firm a breast already flat and fallen.

Time will come tear the mask off of your face;
I will become a swan where black crow was.

55. ELÉGIE

Escoute, Bucheron (arreste un peu le bras)
   Ce ne sont pas des bois que tu jettes à bas,
   Ne vois-tu pas le sang lequel degoute à force
   Des Nymphes qui vivoyent dessous la dure escorce?
Sacrilege meurdrier, si on pend un voleur
   Pour piller un butin de bien peu de valeur,
   Combien de feux, de fers, de morts, & de destresses
   Merites-tu, meschant, pour tuer des Deesses?

Forest, haute maison des oiseaux bocagers,
   Plus le Cerf solitaire & les Chevreuls legers
   Ne paistront sous ton ombre, & ta verte criniere
   Plus du Soleil d'Esté ne rompra la lumiere.

Plus l'amoureux Pasteur sur un tronq adossé,
   Enflant son flageolet à quatre trous persé,
   Son mastin à ses pieds, à son flanc la houlette,
   Ne dira plus l'ardeur de sa belle Janette:
   Tout deviendra muet, Echo sera sans voix:
   Tu deviendras campagne, & en lieu de tes bois,
   Dont l'ombrage incertain lentement se remue,
   Tu sentiras le soc, le coutre & la charrue:
   Tu perdras ton silence, & haletans d'effroy
   Ny satyres ny Pans ne viendront plus chez toy.

Adieu vieille forest, le jouët de Zephyre,
   Où premier j'accorday les langues de ma lyre,
   Où premier j'entendi les fleches resonner
   D'Apollon, qui me vint tout le cœur estonner:
   Où premier admirant la belle Calliope,
   Je devins amoureux de sa neuvaine trope,
   Quand sa main sur le front cent roses me jetta,
   Et de son propre laict Euterpe m'allaita.

. . . Wood butchers, stop in midstroke a moment.
It is not trees you are felling here.
You must see blood gush out of the broken bark;
The living women who inhabit trees
Murdered, defiled. If a thief is hung
For petty larceny, what are you owed:
Fires, manacles, and deaths by torture,
For this purposeful killing of goddesses.

This forest was the high house of thicketing birds.
The solitary buck, the quick roe deer
May not graze from your shadow; your green head
Not break the strands of light from summer sun.
The country lover, backed against a trunk,
Playing his four-hole pipe, his crook laid down,
His mastiff curled against his feet, no longer
Speak his heart's hunger for his lovely Janet.
All will become silence. Echo, voiceless.
The place where trees were, where the uncertain
Shadowings of branches hovered, will be countryside,
Suffer the shock of plow: coulter and share.
Then silence will forsake you, and the goatish
Wilderness people, breathless with fright, not house here.

It was wind, toying with these ancient limbs,
That taught me the language of my first singing.
Here I first heard Apollo's arrows tock
Against the trees; against my amazed heart.
When her hand crowned me with her hundred roses
I loved Calliope here: all the troop of nine.
Euterpe suckled me here at her own breast.

Adieu vieille forest, adieu testes sacrées,
  De tableaux & de fleurs autrefois honorées,
  Maintenant le desdain des passans alterez,
  Qui bruslez en Esté des rayons etherez,
  Saus plus trouver le frais de tes douces verdures,
  Accusent vos meurtriers, & leur disent injures.

Adieu Chesnes, couronne aux vaillans citoyens,
  Arbres de Jupiter, germes Dodonéens,
  Qui premiers aux humains donnastes à repaistre,
  Peuples vrayment ingrats, qui n'ont sceu recognoistre
  Les biens receus de vous, peuples vraiment grossiers,
  De massacrer ainsi nos peres nourriciers.

Que l'homme est malheureux qui au monde se fie!
  O Dieux, que veritable est la Philosophie,
  Qui dit que toute chose à la fin perira.
  Et qu'en changeant de forme une autre vestira:
  De Tempé la vallée un jour sera montagne,
  Et la cyme d'Athos une large campagne,
  Neptune quelquefois de blé sera couvert.
  La matiere demeure, & la forme se perd.

The ancient woods will go. The holy heads.
You were once honored by flowers and votive tablets,
And are disdained now. Summer travelers
Who pass through burning heat, will find no longer
The fresh coolness of your green pleasant branches;
But find your murderers guilty, and so curse them.

The oaks will go: Jupiter's trees, leaf crowns
For brave citizens: the holy speaking seed
Was given by God to humans as their first grain.
They have not recognized your value. They
Are vulgar, indecent, ignorant, ungrateful,
And massacre the fathers who nourished us.

It is a sad man who puts trust in the world.
Philosophy says truly that all things
Will perish finally, and form will change
Material clothing, Salemvria's valley
Will be a mountain top; Mt. Athos, open
Country; Neptune's fields billow with blades of wheat:
For matter lasts, after its form is lost.

56. DES PERES DE FAMILLE
A MONSIEUR S. BLAISE.

Sur le chant, Te rogamus audi nos.

Sainct Blaise, qui vis aux Cieux
    Comme un Ange precieux,
    Si de la terre où nous sommes,
    Tu entens la voix des hommes,
    Recevant les vœuz de tous,
    Je te prie, escoute nous.

Ce jourd'huy que nous faisons
    A ton autel oraisons
    Et processions sacrées
    Pour nous, nos bleds, & nos prées,
    Chantant ton Hynne à genous,
    Je te prie, escoute nous.

Chasse loin de nostre chef
    Toute peste & tout meschef,
    Que l'air corrompu nous verse,
    Quand la main de Dieu diverse
    Respand sur nous son courroux
    Je te prie, escoute nous.

Garde nos petits troupeaux,
    Laines entieres & peux,
    De la ronce dentelée,
    De tac & de clavelée,
    De morfonture & de tous:
    Je te prie, escoute nous,

Que tousjours accompaignez
    Soient de mastins rechignez,
    Le jour allant en pasture,
    Et la nuict en leur closture,
    De peur de la dent des Loups:
    Je te prie, escoute nous

Saint Blaise, you live in the sky
Like a precious angel. If
From this earth where we men are
You will listen to our voices,
Take the vows we offer you
And, I beg you, hear our prayer.

This is your feast day. We make
Holy altar prayers to you
And, parading sacrifice,
For our meadows and prairies,
Sing this hymn upon our knees.
For we beg you, hear our cries.

Keep from falling on our heads
Every mischief, harm, or plague
That corrupted airs downpour
When the angry hand of God
Scatters upon us His ire.
And, I beg you, hear our prayer.

Keep, we beg, our little flocks
Whole of skin and whole of fleece;
From the tooth of bramble free;
From the tick and the sheep pox;
From croup and winter illnesses.
And, I beg you, hear our cries.

While they daily go to grass
Keep the sullen mastiffs back.
Let you keep beside them, where
Locked at night into their folds
You may comfort their wolf-fear.
And, I beg you, hear our prayer.

Si le Loup de sang ardent
   Prend un Mouton en sa dent,
   Quand du bois il sort en queste,
   Huant tous apres la beste,
   Que soudain il soit recous:
   Je te prie, escoute nous.

Garde qu'en allant aux champs,
   Les larrons qui sont meschans,
   Ne desrobent fils ne mere:
   Garde les de la vipere,
   Et d'aspics au ventre rous:
   Je te prie, escoute nous.

Que ny sorcier ny poison
   N'endommagent leur toison
   Par parole ou par bruvage:
   Qu'ils passent l'Esté sans rage,
   Que l'Autonne leur soit dous:
   Je te prie, escoute nous.

Garde nous de trop d'ardeurs,
   Et d'excessives froideurs:
   Donne nous la bonne année,
   Force bleds, force vinée,
   Sans fiebvres, rongne ne clous:
   Je te prie, escoute nous.

Garde nos petits vergers,
   Et nos jardins potagers,
   Nos maisons & nos familles,
   Enfans, & femmes, & filles,
   Et leur donne bons espous:
   Je te prie, escoute nous.

Garde Poulles & Poussins
   De Renards & de larcins:
   Garde sauves nos Avettes,
   Qu'ils portent force fleurettes
   Tousjours en leurs petits trous:
   Je te prie, escoute nous.

If a wolf with urgent blood
Breaks out of the woods in quest
And takes a sheep by surprise,
May the rescue quickly come
Hooting after the great beast,
And, I beg you, hear our cries.

Keep them from evil robber's grasp
When he steals amongst the fields
To rob sons from their mothers.
From the viper protect them,
And from the red bellied asp.
And, I beg you, hear our prayer.

Let no wizard nor poison
By potion nor wicked spell
Cause a damage to their fleece.
Let them not go summer mad;
Let the autumn gentle them.
And, I beg you, hear our cries.

Keep in health our orchard trees,
And our kitchen gardens fair;
Our houses wives and families,
Our sons and daughters in your care.
Bring them worthy marriages.
And, I beg you, hear our prayer

Keep us from too strong a heat;
Keep us from excessive cold
And send us the best of years.
Force the wheat and fruit the vine;
Save us from fever, scab, and rot.
And, I beg you, hear our cries.

Keep our hens and little chicks
From pilferage, and from the fox.
Keep our honey bees in care.
See they carry many bags
Of pollen to their little hives.
And, I beg you, hear our prayer.

Fay naistre force boutons
   Pour engraisser nos Moutons,
   Et force fueille menue,
   Que paist la troupe cornue
   De nos Chévres & nos Boucs:
   Je te prie, escoute nous.

Chasse la guerre bien loing:
   Romps les armes dans le poing
   Du soldat qui frappe & tue
   Celuy qui tient la charrue,
   Mangeant son bien en deux coups:
   Je te prie, escoute nous.

Que le plaideur grippe-tout
   Par procez qui sont sans bout,
   N'enveloppe le bon homme,
   Qui chiquanant se consomme,
   Puis meurt de faim & de pous:
   Je te prie, escoute nous.

Que l'impudent usurier,
   Laissant l'interest premier,
   N'assemble point sans mesure
   Usure dessus usure,
   Pour ravir son petit clous:
   Je te prie, escoute nous.

Garde nos petits ruisseaux
   De souillure de Pourceaux,
   Naiz pour engrasser leur pance:
   Pour eux tombe en abondance
   Le Glan des Chesnes secous:
   Je te prie, escoute nous.

Nos Genices au Printemps
   Ne sentent Mousches ne Tans:
   Enflent de laict leurs mamelles:
   Que pleines soient nos faicelles
   De fourmages secs & mous:
   Je te prie, escoute nous.

Bring out buds in the meadows
To give fatness to our sheep;
And cause slender leaves to rise
So that our horned flocks may graze,
All our billygoats and does;
And, I beg you, hear our cries.

Keep us well away from war.
Break the weapons from the fists
Of soldiers who kill those who are
Plowmen, and who then take two
Bites to eat their wealth and stock.
And, I beg you, hear our prayer.

Let the grasping plaintiff, with
All his endless court proceedings,
Not wrap honest men in lies.
Let his own tricks eat him. Give
Death by hunger and by lice.
And, I beg you, hear our cries.

Let the impudent usurer
Losing his first interest
Not assemble limitless
Usury on usury
To delight his little hoard.
And, I beg you, hear our prayer.

Keep our little rivers sweet,
Free from the manure of pigs.
Swell their stomachs up with grease.
Send them abundant harvests of
Acorns shaken from oak trees.
And, I beg you, hear our cries.

Let our heifers in the Spring
Feel no horsefly nor housefly.
With milk make their bags full and fair
That our hanging baskets fill
With cheeses that are soft and dry.
And, I beg you, hear our prayer.

Nos Bouviers sans murmurer
    Puissent la peine endurer,
    Bien repeus à nostre table:
    Soient les Bœufs dedans l'estable
    Tousjours de fourrages saouls:
    Je te prie, escoute nous.

Chasse loin les paresseux:
    Donne bon courage à ceux
    Qui travaillent, sans blesseure
    De congnées, & sans morseure
    De Chiens enragez & fous:
    Je te prie, escoute nous.

Bref, garde nous de terreurs,
    Et de Paniques fureurs,
    Et d'illusion estrange,
    Et de feu sacré, qui mange
    Membres, arteres, & pouls:
    Je te prie, escoute nous.

Donne que ceux qui viendront
    Prier ton nom, & tendront
    A ton autel leurs offrandes,
    Jouyssent de leurs demandes
    De tous leurs pechez absous:
    Je te prie, escoute nous.

Sainct Blaise, qui vis aux Cieux
    Comme un Ange precieux,
    Si de la terre où nous sommes,
    Tu entens la voix des hommes,
    Recevant las vœuz de tous,
    Je te prie, escoute nous.

Let our herders bear their work,
Manage without murmuring.
At our tables give them ease;
So may the oxen in their stalls
Ever have their bellyfull.
And, I beg you, hear our cries.

Keep idle men away from us.
Give good courage without hard
Knocks to those who labor here.
Let them not suffer the bite
Dogs enraged with madness give.
And, I beg you, hear our prayer.

In short, save us from terror.
Save us from the panic rage,
From the snares of foreign lies,
From the holy gnawing flame
Of limbs and pulse and arteries.
And, I beg you, hear our cries.

Grant that those who come to you,
Call your name, and to you bring
Altar gifts, may find you there.
Give our requests fruitfulness
And absolve us of our sins.
And, I beg you, hear our prayer.

Saint Blaise, you live in the sky
Like a precious angel. If
From this earth where we men are
You will listen to our voices,
Take the vows we offer you
And, I beg you, hear our prayer.

57.

Je n'ay plus que les os, un Schelette je semble,
  Decharné, denervé, demusclé, depoulpé,
  Que le trait de la mort sans pardon a frappé,
  Je n'ose voir mes bras que de peur je ne tremble.

Apollon & son filz deux grans maistres ensemble,
  Ne me sçauroient guerir, leur mestier m'a trompé,
  Adieu plaisant soleil, mon œil est estoupé,
  Mon corps s'en va descendre où tout se desassemble.

Quel amy me voyant en ce point despouillé
  Ne remporte au logis un œil triste & mouillé,
  Me consolant au lict & me baisant la face,

En essuiant mes yeux par la mort endormis?
  Adieu chers compaignons, adieu mes chers amis,
  Je m'en vay le premier vous preparer la place.

I am nothing but bones. I am my skeleton
Unfleshed: nerve, muscle, pulp, all taken
Without pardon, by death's stroke.
And I am left afraid to look on my own shaking arms.

Apollo and his son, the two grand masters,
Working together, could not heal this. Healing has failed me;
And all my body settles to its disassembling.

A friend who sees me flayed to this
Will bring sad eyes and weeping to the house, and lean
To comfort me on my bed, and kiss

To test my eyes for being made asleep
By death. You are my friends, my good companions.
I must go before you to make your rooms ready.

58.

Meschantes nuicts d'hyver, nuicts filles de Cocyte
   Que la terre engendra d'Encelade les seurs,
   Serpentes d'Alecton, & fureur des fureurs,
   N'aprochez de mon lict, ou bien tournez plus vitte.

Que fait tant le soleil au gyron d'Amphytrite?
   Leve toy, je languis accablé de douleurs,
   Mais ne pouvoir dormir c'est bien de mes malheurs
   Le plus grand, qui ma vie & chagrine & despite.

Seize heures pour le moins je meur les yeux ouvers,
   Me tournant, me virant de droit & de travers,
   Sus l'un sus l'autre flanc je tempeste, je crie,

Inquiet je ne puis en un lieu me tenir,
   J'appelle en vain le jour, & la mort je supplie,
   Mais elle fait la sourde, & ne veut pas venir.

The sun lost in sea weave: Hell's river's daughters,
Avenging serpents, nights of ghastly fury,
Winter nights: keep from my bed
Black daughters, or turn, turn more quickly,

Bring the sun back. I lie harassed by pain.
The power of sleep is taken—that greatest
Of my illnesses, troubles, insults my life.
I die with my eyes open, turning and tacking.

For sixteen hours at least I storm
From one side to another, crying,
And cannot keep myself quietly to one place.

I call day vainly, and I plead with death
While she fakes deafness; keeps her distance.

59.

Il faut laisser maisons & vergers & jardins,
  Vaisselles & vaisseaux que l'artisan burine,
  Et chanter son obseque en la façon du Cygne,
  Qui chante son trespas sur les bors Mæandrins.

C'est fait j'ay devidé le cours de mes destins,
  J'ay vescu j'ay rendu mon nom assez insigne,
  Ma plume vole au ciel pour estre quelque signe
  Loin des appas mondains qui trompent les plus fins.

Heureux qui ne fut onc, plus heureux qui retourne
  En rien comme il estoit, plus heureux qui sejourne
  D'homme fait nouvel ange aupres de Jesuchrist,

Laissant pourrir ça bas sa despouille de boüe
  Dont le sort, la fortune, & le destin se joüe,
  Franc des liens du corps pour n'estre qu'un esprit.

He must abandon houses, orchards, gardens,
The vessels marked by the engraver,
And sing his funeral. The swan sings his own funeral on the Meander's margin.

It is finished. I have come to the end of my destiny,
And lived. I made my name remarkable enough.
My words should hang in the air like a bird made of stars,
Far from the world's bait.

Happy who never was. Happier who returns
To nothing as he was. Happier who lives
New angel, made of man, by Jesus Christ.

So let this muddy hide rot out,
Whose lot both destiny and fortune gambled over.
Be spirit only. Let the body be.

60.

A son ame.

Amelette Ronsardelette,
  Mignonnelette doucelette,
  Treschere hostesse de mon corps,
  Tu descens là bas foiblelette,
  Pasle, maigrelette, seulette,
  Dans le froid Royaume des mors:
  Toutesfois simple, sans remors
  De meurtre, poison, ou rancune,
  Méprisant faveurs & tresors
  Tant enviez par la commune.

Passant, j'ay dit, suy ta fortune
  Ne trouble mon repos, je dors.

Darling, my body's hostess,
Little soul, little Ronsard's
Darling; my most delicate:
You will go down then, white
And a little lonesome
Slenderness, into the cold kingdom
Of the dead—all simple still,
Without remorse or rancor
For murder, poison—
Mistrusting wealth and favor,
So longed for by your fellows.
Ladies and gentlemen, my talk
Is finished: follow your
Fortune. Don't trouble
My rest. I will sleep now.

NOTES

The French texts are taken from the *Oeuvres complètes*, ed. P. Laumonier; edition completed by I. Silver and R. Lebègue (Paris, 1914–1967), 18 volumes.

Except where the notes specifically indicate the contrary, therefore, the text offered represents the earliest published version of the poem. Each poem is identified by its title, by its first line where necessary, and by the date and title of the first collection within which it was published. Finally, each poem is identified by the volume and page number in the Laumonier edition (abbreviated L.).

1. A CHARLES DE PISSELEU EVESQUE DE CONDON
Quatre premiers livres des Odes (1550), III, 1
L. II, 1

excerpt (lines 49–60)

The majority of the ode is a carefully antique discussion, drawn largely from Horace and Virgil, about the inconstancy of human dedication. The verse is formal and grave as fits the circumstance of its composition. It is essentially an application to a potential patron, the bishop of Condon. The final stanzas give a romanticized but at the same time probably quite genuine version of Ronsard's vision of his trade.

Line 2. *Euterpe*, one of the muses, is the patron of music, and also the inventor of the flute and other wind instruments. Ronsard originally intended much of his verse to be actually sung; and he felt himself to be working in the Greek and Roman tradition of lyric poetry, which assumed that verse would be sung; or, if read only, would be read as if the music were missing.

Line 3. *Common pretenders* takes the place of *le vulgaire odieus*, the French version of the Latin *profanum vulgus*, the group so carefully avoided by Horace, Virgil, Livy. The adjective *odieus* comes from the Horatian phrase, *Odi profanum vulgus*, "I hate the uninitiated crowd." The "vulgus" should not be confused with the "common man," particularly the honest workman, whom the Roman poets, and Ronsard, professed to admire. The statement has nothing to do with class distinction, but rather with singling out for ridicule those whose pretensions make their noninitiation plain.

Line 9. Euterpe's baptizing represents a mingling of the Christian and the Classical that is typical not only of Ronsard's technique but of the general tradition within which he was working. The act immediately calls up an echo of Achilles' inundation in the Styx by his mother Thetis. However, the act, being called baptism, is a reference to that Christian sacrament. At the same time priests are not baptized, they are ordained by bishops (a fact of which Charles de Pisseleu had reason to be aware). The act of baptizing makes Euterpe a Christian by retrospect, and clears the way for Ronsard to become a classical myth.

2. A LA FORÊT DE GASTINE
Quatre premiers livres des Odes (1550), II, 23
L. I, 243
Text of 1578 and 1584

The forest of Gastine was a part of Ronsard's inheritance. For generations Ronsards had been wardens, or *Sergents fieffés*, of the forest, which belonged to the Counts of Vendôme. The forest was on the southern bank of the Loir. Henri de Bourbon, king of Navarre and duke of Vendôme, had a large part of the forest cut for cash some thirty years after this ode was composed. The poem that concerns that sacrilege will be found later in the selection (55).

Line 4. *Erymanthus* is a mountain, river, or town of Arcadia, or Arcadia itself. Hercules killed his large boar in these parts.

Line 10. *amazed.* Ronsard's *Ravi d'esprit* suggests the common acceptance of the notion, drawn from Plato's early dialogue, the *Ion*, that the poet must speak the truth, because inspired by higher powers who speak through his mouth. This is the Bacchic notion of poetic madness. Plato makes a careful distinction between the mere craftsmen (whose equivalents among Ronsard's contemporaries would be the *Rhétoriqueurs*) and those, like Pindar, through whom divine force really speaks. This Platonic backing may in part be responsible for Ronsard's respect for, and imitation of, Pindar.

Line 12. *frankly.* Ronsard's "I deliver myself all *franc* (free) from evil care." I have in my mind the strong echo of Gerard's preface to his *Herball* (London, 1597): "Although my paines have not been spent (courteous Reader) in the gracious discoverie of golden mynes . . . yet hath my labour (I trust) beene otherwise profitably imployed, in descrying of such harmlesse treasure of herbes, trees and plants, as the earth frankly without violence offereth unto our most necessarie uses."

3. A CUPIDON POUR PUNIR JANNE CRUELLE
Quatre premiers livres des Odes (1550), II, 19
L. II, 51

excerpt (lines 1–20)

The entire ode is a vigorous weaving of themes from Horace, Petrarch, Ovid, Pontano—and becomes a sly suggestion that Cupid should leave Ronsard to his high causes, and instead take on Janne, whose lack of responsiveness has made her deserve punishment.

4. DE LA VENUE DE L'ESTÉ AU SEIGNEUR DE BONNIVET EVESQUE DE BESIERS
Quatre premiers livres des Odes (1550), III, 10
L. II, 23

The text is that of 1550, with the exception of lines 67 (var. 55–84), 82–84 (var. 67–84). Line 54, "Their sides heaving with heat," translates the variant of 1584 for line 66, *"Rebattant leurs flancs de chaleur."* To have included that line in the text presented here would either have violated the rhyme scheme, or else would have committed me to the inclusion of what seems an unfortunate companion to the 1584 variant, where lines 62 and 63 were changed to read *"Où les fonteines emperlées De fleurs remirent la couleur."*

Bonnivet was bishop of Besiers from October 1546 to December 1547. As Laumonier points out, this allows the poem to be given a date of June or July of 1547.

Line 6. *The Dog Star. Canicule, Canicula,* or *Sirius.* The following stanza is a series of astronomical statements. Ronsard's astronomy, though elementary, is firm in its adherence to the time's most conservative and respectable assumption: that the earth sat quietly in the center of a series of concentric spheres that were the universe. The sun moved in a different plane from the stars and according to a different pattern. Consequently, the sun's rising and setting coincided at different times, with different constellations.

The sun, as the first created light, is the origin of all light, and of fire and heat, which are among light's accidental qualities. The star's light, according at least to some systems, is reflected (or in some other way copied) from the sun: and the proximity of a star to the sun is responsible for the amount of heat engendered. Thus, when Sirius coincides with the sun, the heat of the earth is severely augmented. Cancer is of course the Crab, the sign that presides over the end of June and the beginning of July. One story has this constellation be the dog of Erigone, and her eternal companion.

Line 28. *flowers that Apollo takes.* The French, *les fleurs Apollinées,* Laumonier suggests to be Ronsard's echo of Virgil's *Paeoniae herbae* (*Aeneid,* VII, 769) and Ovid's *Apollineae medicamen prolis* (*Metamorphoses,* XV, 533). This identifies the flowers only as being available for medicinal use—Apollo being the father of medicine; Paean being Apollo's son, and the doctor who brought Hippolytus back to life through herb lore.

Line 29. *Adonis. Adonis aestivalis,* is sometimes found growing in wheatfields in Europe. It resembles the anemone. Gerard gives it the latin name *Flos Adonis flore rubro.* The flower is mentioned here not for any medicinal property (Gerard says only that people have recently begun to use it for the colic), but because it does, for a fact, bloom through May, June, July, and into August; and because it brings with it the legend of Adonis, whom Venus loved, who was killed by a boar, and from whose blood the flower sprang.

Line 44. *Erigone* the daughter of Icarius, hung herself after learning of the death of her father, who had been killed by some shepherds whom he had intoxicated. She became the constellation Virgo, through which the sun moves in July and August. She is described in Ovid (*Met.* X) as being "raised to heaven by her devoted love of her father." That, and the occurrence of this passage in the midst of the story of Myrrha, who having despaired of finding a way to sleep with her father, hanged herself, but was cut down in time by her nurse and helped to achieve that desire, during the annual festival of Ceres; makes it seem that Ronsard is recalling and mixing the two stories. It is particularly interesting that the passage, a few lines earlier in the same book, that introduces the story of Myrrha, (". . . other animals mate without any discrimination; there is no shame for a heifer in having her father mount her, a horse takes his own daughter to wife, goats mate with the she-goats they have sired . . ."), have surely influenced Ronsard's lines 41 and 71–73). The quotations from Ovid are taken from Mary Innes's fine translation, *The Metamorphoses of Ovid* (Baltimore, 1961), p. 254, 258.

5. A DIEU POUR LA FAMINE
Bocage (1552), IX
L. II, 184

The occasion for this poem was the great famine of 1546. It is inspired also by Clément Marot's translations from the Psalms, a highly influential group of poems, published in 1540, which did a good deal to make the French language appear a fit receptacle for inherited culture, and an eloquent and suitable medium for formal important poetry. In Ronsard's time Latin was still assumed to be the proper language in which to couch such sentiments. I will quote a small bit of Marot's *Psalm 23*, because its form will be seen to influence Ronsard's; and its language, I suspect, has something to do with Ronsard's approach to an ode like his Ode to Summer (4).

Mon Dieu me paist soubz sa puissance haulte,
C'est mon berger, de rien je n'auray faulte.
En tect bien seur, joignant les beaulx herbages,
Coucher me faict, me mene aux clairs rivages,
Traicte ma vie en doulceur trèshumaine,
Et pour son nom par droictz sentiers me meine . . .
Clément Marot, *Oevres Complètes* ed. Grenier
(Paris, /1951?/), II, 341.

Ronsard's rhyme and meter read rather lumpily, and Dassonville, in his study *Ronsard, Etude historique et littéraire* (Geneva, 1968), I, 162, assigns this to youthful ineptitude. However, if one imagines the psalm sung to a rousing processional, its character at once improves.

Line 55. *Scyths, Tartars, and the Turks.* The Turkish Ottoman Empire had begun expansion into Hungary in 1526, invaded Austria in 1529 and 1532 (they were set back at Vienna in 1529); at the time of this poem's writing, the Ottoman Empire, under Suleiman the Magnificent, reached as far as Algeria, Hungary, the Persian Gulf, and Aden, and looked exceedingly healthy. The Tartars, or Mongols, were on the decline. The Khanate of the Golden Horde, which had penetrated as far as the eastern borders of the German Empire in the late thirteenth century, had disintegrated in 1502 (by which time it had been driven back to the north and west of the Black

Sea). But the Mongols had been demanding neighbors, and must
have been vividly remembered for many years. The Scyths, who
were a real people, a horse culture to the north of the Black Sea,
were already vague and rather legendary in Herodotus's time; and
by the time Virgil was writing about them, the name seems to
have applied to Mongols, or perhaps to barbarians in general. This
passage, therefore, mixes current events with classical allusions.

Line 62. *The Age of Gold.* A Roman version of the myth of Paradise made a
legend that had people living without labor, eating what the earth
produced naturally, and without ambition. (Another Roman ver-
sion of the age of Gold makes it Saturn's period of kingship over
the Italians, during which time he taught them the arts of agri-
culture.) This was a popular theme in the French Renaissance, and
an important theme in Ronsard's earlier thinking. See Elizabeth
Armstrong, *Ronsard and the Age of Gold* (Cambridge, 1968).
Ronsard is drawing an obvious parallel between the gift of manna,
and the gift of acorns. But there is also a strong moral concern
here, in that the idea of the superiority of the completely simple
(or natural) life of the "savage" (not, obviously, the "barbarian")
is being considered. In times of desperate famine, acorns did serve
as food for humans, although they were normally assigned to the
use of pigs, who were allowed to roam through woods in their
natural state of innocence (see 56).

6. *Qui voudra voir comme un Dieu me surmonte*
Les Amours (1552), I
L. IV, 5

This is the opening sonnet of the sequence with which Ronsard sets out,
with rather open calculation, to do for French poetry what Petrarch had done
for Italian. In 1552 the sonnet was not a customary French form. Ronsard
adopted it, taking it from the Italian model and, over the course of many
years, made it his most powerful medium. The use of the Petrarchan sonnet
is important for Ronsard in that it provides a vehicle for, simultaneously, a
correct and well-defined logical arrangement of ideas, and an act of self-
examination. Presumably the self-examination in these first efforts is not as
genuine, or as fruitful, as it becomes in the later sonnets. But the exercise of
logical intelligence, and the widening scope of reference to which Ronsard
begins to address himself, are important. This poem talks about contradictions,
and about love's tyranny over both emotion and intellect. In Ronsard's love
poetry, except where he specifically tells us otherwise, it seems the safest course
to assume that he is working abstractly rather than with any attempt at
autobiography.

7. *Je veulx darder par l'univers ma peine*
Les Amours (1552), XVI
L. IV, 19

Lines 5–11. This is the first occurrence, in this selection, of the theme of metamorphosis. Ronsard was influenced considerably not merely by the stories in Ovid's *Metamorphoses* but more by their ability to present vivid, pregnant, and active metaphor. Although the origin of Ronsard's metamorphic theme appears to be classical, Catholic orthodoxy, as it entrenched itself against systems of Protestant thinking that held a majority of the good scientific cards, maintained for a long time a description of material behavior that allowed metamorphisis to be believed in, at least as a possibility. What was at stake was the defense of the doctrine of transubstantiation, the description of the physical process by which bread and wine became the body and blood of Christ in the sacrament of the Eucharist. The Jesuit R. P. Maldonat's *Traicte Des Anges et Demons,* mis en français par Maistre François de la Borie grand Archidiacre et Chanoine à Perigueux (Paris, 1605), devotes a chapter to the question of whether bodies can be changed into various forms by demons. He compares those who make fun of Ovid's *Metamorphoses* to the Calvinists when they deny transubstantiation: and drawing on the authority of Ovid, Homer, Theocritus, Virgil, Pliny, Fabius, Agriopas, Pomponius Mela, Apuleius, Saint Augustine, Lucian—he argues that demons can, in fact, transmute one body to another, and that in three manners (pp. 214 ff).

Essential to this sort of discussion is the division, which we will see more clearly later in Ronsard, between matter and form. This is the Scholastic rendering of Aristotle's explanation of matter. The Schoolmen spoke as if matter and form (or accident and substance) could exist independently of each other. And the world, when Ronsard comes to examine it philosophically, seems to be a sort of ferris wheel of undefined matter passing through another ferris wheel of defined form, producing a third ferris wheel of discrete objects— and all this in some way corresponding to, or defined by, the great interconnecting ferris wheels of sun, stars, and planets.

It is impossible to say how much of all of this Ronsard genuinely believed at any point. But it cannot be emphasized too much that what look, to us, like the most irresponsible beliefs (including astrology, magic), were in fact in Ronsard's time, the most orthodox, conservative, and pious.

Lines 12–14. A mingling of themes and legends. If the flower is to be born of Ronsard's color on the river, it should be done by reflection. If that is the case, the reference is to Narcissus, who fell in love with his own reflection, failed to persuade his reflection to return his affections, killed himself, and had a flower grow from his blood. Gerard identifies the Narcissus intended by Ovid in his telling of the story (*Metamorphosis* III) as either (or both) *Narcissus medio purpureus*, Purple circled Daffodil; or *Narcissus medio purpureus praecox*, Timely purple ringed daffodil. If it is this flower to which Ronsard refers, the being painted with his injury (*de mon mal soit peinte*), is explained. Laumonier suggests that it is the Hyacinth to which Ronsard is alluding. (Gerard identifies it as the *Hyacinthus orientalis caeruleus*, or blew Oriental Iacint.) Hyacinth was a boy whom Apollo loved and killed accidentally. The flower grew from his blood, and its leaves bore the letters A I, which Apollo printed there as a testament to his mourning. If it is this flower Ronsard has in mind, the being painted with his name (*de mon nom soit peinte*) is explained.

Laumonier suggests also that the tercet is an allusion to the symbol Ronsard's father, Loys, adopted for himself. He had campaigned in Italy, and, under Italian influence, remade his small Manor, *La Possonière*, and invented a new coat of arms—burning roses (des *ronces* qui *ardent*)—to take the place of the three parallel fish (*ronces*) to which his family inheritance entitled him.

8. *Je vouldroy bien richement jaunissant*
Les Amours (1552), XX
L. IV, 23

Lines 1–4. Reference to the story of Danaë.

Line 5. I have adopted the variant of 1560–1572, which substitutes *blanchissant* for *blandissant*. Ronsard's reference is to the rape of Europa.

Lines 9–11. The Narcissus story is twisted, and made more fruitful, by the suggestion that the water into which the speaker looks be a separate individual, and receptive. *Cassandre* is Cassandre Salviati, the daughter of a wealthy Florentine banker, who in 1546 had married a neighbor of the Ronsards in the vicinity of Couture, Vendômois, the Seigneur de Pray, but whom Ronsard continued to court, at least so far as the publication of poems addressed to her can be called courting. The fact is that one could not write this sort of poem without either having, or pretending to have, an object for them.

9. *Plus tost le bal de tant d'astres divers*
Les Amours (1552), XXVI
L. IV, 29

This is one of many sonnets in *Les Amours* whose argument depends on Ronsard's vague, but generous, cosmology. The ponderous organ music of the opening six lines, leading to what seems anticlimactical, may reduce the force of what we guess to be Ronsard's intention. But we who have been schooled in the sonnet as practiced by Milton and Wordsworth are prepared only for the Cosmic and Humorless. Ronsard's intention is gay and argumentative.

Line 1. *The dance of the stars,* Ronsard's version of the Greek Χόρος ἀστρῶν. Elsewhere (10) he names the dance as a *Branle,* which Huguet defines as a *danse de plusieurs personnes se tenant par le main.* It is a fixed system of a number of bodies which move in patterns that are ordained.

Lines 2–3. Reference is made here (and is continued in the sonnet that follows this one in the selection) to a mixing of the Greek creation myth, and that to be found in Genesis. In the beginning was Chaos. Chaos was either a Greek god, or a formless, undefined wealth of material, or "the water" over which the Spirit of God, or the Sun, or Amor, moved, causing it to divide. Thus the element of fire (the sun, the extension of, or image of, the Spirit of God), moving over the element of water, and working upon it, caused the generation of the other two elements—air, which was rarefied water; and earth, which was water out of which the air had been rarefied.

The great All (Ronsard's *Tout*) is the Spirit of God, or else its Greek equivalent. The theme is developed much more carefully in *Le Chat* (39 in this selection). This is not a pantheism, but a system in which all parts share the same origin and nature, and so correspond to each other in intelligible ways. Ronsard is saying that the system will go into reverse and reproduce Chaos before he loves a blonde and green-eyed lady.

Line 4. The universe Ronsard imagines has a spherical outer edge (he describes it as an egg, L. XVII, 334). Ronsard's *abymes ouverts* would be the empty void beyond that, which it would make no sense to think of as being animated. Since we imagine our universe (if at all) to be a different shape from Ronsard's, I've substituted our Black Holes for his open abyss.

Line 13. *image.* Laumonier points out that Ronsard's *Idée* should be taken here to mean not the *Idea* of the Platonist, but the image which a seen thing prints on the soul.

10. *Avant qu'Amour, du Chaos otieux*
Les Amours (1552), XLII

> Lempriere (writing in 1788) accepts the unlikely bit of literary history that Ronsard seems to assume: "CHAOS, a rude and shapeless mass of matter . . . from which the universe was formed by the hand and power of a superior being. This doctrine was first established by Hesiod . . . and it is probable that it was obscurely drawn from the account of Moses, by being copied from the annals of Sanchoniathon, whose age is fixed antecedent to the siege of Troy."

Line 1. *inert.* Ronsard uses the adjective *otieux* frequently, with a number of different meanings. It can mean, as it does here, simply inert; it can carry a pejorative tone and mean lazy or idle; it can carry a tone of moral approbation and mean simple.

Lines 8–13. Denys l'Areopagite (*De nominibus divinis*, I) describes an atomic system which Ronsard is here using. In this system (which depends heavily on Lucretius) the soul is made up of atoms in the same way that matter is; and the soul reflects, or imitates, the circular or spheroidal movement to be found throughout the universe.

11. *Je veus brusler pour m'en voler aux cieux*
Les Amours (1552), CXXXIX
L. IV, 134

Lines 1–2. The opening sentiment reflects a continuance of the description of the material world within which Ronsard is working. The idea of being set fire to by love is of course already hoary when Ronsard comes to it—it is the Italian version of the neo-Platonic poetic description of what Love can do to the soul. The flaming of your eyes (line 8) is a usual enough source of ignition.

"Je veus brusler . . . tout l'imparfait" represents a theory still being stubbornly defended as late as 1674. Jean Baptiste Fayol, Prieur Commendataire de Notre-Dame de Donges, in an astronomical work, *L'Harmonie Celeste, Decouvrant les Diverses Dispositions de la Nature* (Paris, 1674), a work designed to refute the errors of Descartes, one of the greatest of which was the idea that the earth moved around the sun—describes the nature of the four elements. The sun, he says (p. 42), is light which is pure, and which does not manifest the accidents of heat and flame. For impurity is the sole cause of inflammation (*L'impureté est la seule cause de l'inflammation*). He says further that one could stand at the center of the sun and not burn there.

Line 3. *Alcmene's son.* Hercules.

Line 14. *The other loveliness.* Ronsard is entrenched in the late *amour courtois* tradition. That tradition celebrated a chaste (our commonly used adjective *platonic*) relationship, sometimes made spicier by lapses, in which the perfection of the female beloved was seen to be a reflection of, and invitation toward, the perfection (God) which had created it.

The sonnet that immediately follows this one in *Les Amours* (CXL), continues the theme of flight, but brings it back rudely to the sublunary world, by referring to the fable of Icarus.

12. FOLASTRIE
Livret de folastrie (1553), IV
L, V, 30

This is a playful mockery of more serious country romances by other poets, and a friendly recollection and mockery of their classical sources. It is the one example I have chosen from an entire book that Ronsard published the year after *Les Amours*, which some suggest to be intended as an answer to critics who claimed his concerns in the earlier book were too deep, hard, and complicated. Ronsard wrote plenty of his own remarkably serious pastorals later, and another, *Le Voyage de Tours*, one of his most successful poems, which tilts back and forth on the fence between the serious and the friendly, is included later in this selection (36).

Line 24. *The lonesome valley . . .* Ronsard's *valées closes* presumably means to recall, and incriminate as it were, Petrarch's beloved Vaucluse.

Line 30. *stems of hemp.* Ronsard's *chenevotes* are bits of *chanvre*, known also under its Latin name *cannabis. The Jardin de Santé* (Paris, 1539), opens its discussion of the operations of the plant by referring to Pliny's authority that the seed of hemp is said to extend a man's generative capacity; to which should be added the further information (taken from Galen) that the plant has so drying a quality that, if too much of it be eaten, it dries up the seed. (Gerard points out this fact.) Rabelais gives a most interesting and useful discussion of the plant, which he calls Pantagruelion (*The Histories of Gargantua and Pantagruel*, Book III, chaps. 50–52), in which he includes the information that the stalks of the plant are commonly used for fuel. Rabelais does not mention—nor do Gerard or the author of the *Jardin de Santé*—the possibility that the leaves might also serve as fuel, as they are sometimes known to do under the Spanish name for the same plant, *marijuana.*

fougeres. Of the many plants which we call "ferns," the sixteenth-century herbals single out, as being referred to by what has become that generic name, two in specific, the *Filix-mas, Male Ferne,* or *Fougère Masle* (*Polysticum Filix-mas*); and *Felix fœmina, Female ferne* or *brakes* (*Athyrium Filix-femina*). The root of the fern is used medicinally; and among its virtues is the ability to expel worms, and (this is particularly the province of the female fern) to prevent women from conceiving.

Line 31. Ronsard's *Tramble*, the *Peuplier Tremble* (*Populus Tremula*) is identified by Gerard as the *Populus Lybica*, or *Aspen*, and in the *Jardin de Santé* as that species of poplar called *limbica*. According to the *Jardin de Santé*, the leaves, when drunk, prevent conception (*Les feuilles dicelluy beues apres la purgation des menstrues par semblable maniere empesche & ne laisse point concevoir*). Gerard reports that ". . . The same barke is also reported to make a woman barren, if it be drunke with the kidney of a mule, which thing the leaves likewise are thought to performe, being taken after the flowers or reds be ended."

Line 40. *smock*. Ronsard's word *sein* means sometimes lap, sometimes bosom; and from time to time in his emendations he changes it to the alternate word *giron*, which also means either bosom or lap. But I have taken the word in this case to be more aptly translated by an article of clothing, as suggested by Ronsard himself in his note to the word *sein* as used in the *Franciade* (I, 116; L. XVI, 36). *C'est ce que disent les Latins SINUS: c'estoit une piece de drap ou d'autre semblable matiere, large et longue, pliée, cousue et entée a la robe, en la partie qui est devant l'estomac, qu'ils retroussoient par dessus l'espaule dextre, et du bout s'en couvroient la teste, car ils ne portoient pas de bonnet.* A smock seemed the closest thing a shepherdess might have to such an article of clothing.

Line 41. Ronsard's *buret* is identified by Silver, in his addition to Laumonier's notes on this poem (L. XIX, 59), as the diminutive of *bur* or *bis*. Olivier de Serres (*Le Théâtre d'Agriculture et Mesnage des Champs* (Paris, 1600), p. 826, describes *pain bis* as made for the household *"grossiers,"* or louts, and laborers. Depending on the condition of the harvest, it can be made of whole wheat (in good times) or barley, millet, oats, even of acorns in time of famine. It has the advantage that it will keep for several weeks. It can be fed to dogs and pigs, particularly when made largely of chaff.

Line 42. *Le Jardin de Santé* describes oats as a food for beasts of burden, and not humans, unless hunger drives them to make bread of it. Our shepherdess's delicacy is thus described for certain.

Line 44. *garlic*. Le Jardin de Santé: *Quant il est broye avecques coriandre verte il incite luxure*. (It incites luxury when it is crushed with green coriander.) Gerard: ". . . it engendreth naughtie and sharpe blood. Therefore such as are of a hot complexion must especially abstain from it." Leeks (line 45) have a similar reputation.

Line 56. *hillock.* Ronsard's *motte.* Huguet defines *Motte* as *"colline, eminence, lieu elevé."* I would point out this couplet of Ronsard's "Les mottes enfant'ront en lieu de bleds germez / Une fiere moisson de chevaliers armés." *Hymne de Calais, et de Zetes,* 1. 607–608: L. VIII, 287.

Line 59. The architecture of the rose was one element that contributed to its wide applicability as a symbol. Although it has medical properties, a number of which are related to the heart, those values seem not to be at issue here. Rather its form. The final section of Dante's *Divina Comedia* comes to mind, as does also the main reading room of the Library of Congress, whose concentric rings of unfurled desks seem to have been planned by someone familiar with the sort of imagery Ronsard is using here.

Line 62. *hobble.* Ronsard's *tribart* is a stick of wood which can have either of two purposes. It can be used as a hobble to prevent the speedy movement of a horse or cow, when attached between the legs or, when fastened to the neck of pigs, calves, dogs, it prevents them from running through hedges, fences.

Line 75. *cover.* Ronsard's *jauche,* (from the word *jau,* cock) is a countryman's term for the rooster's servicing of the hen.

Line 76. *dibble.* Ronsard's *pau* probably means post.

13. ODE A CASSANDRE
Les Amours, appendice (1553)
L. V, 196

The sonnet begins as a song, and under Petrarch's tutelage, becomes a vehicle for sung logic. This song (not a sonnet, actually, but close in shape) is Ronsard's manner of continuing the logical structure of the sung poem. The logical structure and purpose of this poem are carefully discussed by Donald Stone Jr., *Ronsard's Sonnet Cycles: a study in tone and vision* (New Haven, 1966).

As Silver points out (L. XIX, 64), this ode was published some seven years after the marriage of Cassandre Salviati. His words do not invite argument *"Il est très peu probable qu'elle ait été réellement écrite pour la dame de Pray: le nom de Cassandre n'est qu'un prétexte à exercise poétique."*

The theme is ancient, and remains constant in Ronsard's thinking.

14. ÉPITRE A AMBROISE DE LA PORTE PARISIEN
Bocage (1554)
L. VI, 10

This is the first poem to which Ronsard gave the title *Epistle*.

Line 1. Laumonier assigns this poem to the Autumn of 1553, when the plague raged in Paris.

Line 8. *Meaux*. Ronsard had been given a benefice (that is to say, an ecclesiastically derived income), from *Mareuil-les-Meux*.

Line 11. *The wine of Ay (Aï)*. Le Paulmier, in 1588, wrote as follows: *"le vin d'Aï . . . est de déliée et subtile matière, plaisant à boire, de facile digestion et de prompte distribution, qui fait que les roys et princes en font souvent leur breuvage ordinaire."* Cited in Roger Dion, *Histoire de la vigne et du vin en France des origines au XIXᵉ siècle* (Paris, 1959), p. 627. It was one of the oldest and most honored of the *grands crus* of the *Ile-de-France*.

Line 16. *Shepherd Apollo*. Apollo was supposed to have spent nine years tending the flocks of Admetus.

Line 23. *Hills terraced in vineyards*. Ronsard's *"colines pamprées"* means grape-vined hills.

Line 33. *cancrous*. Ronsard is referring to the crablike pincer that the crayfish (*écrevisse*) carries.

Line 39. *the lines Virgil had Tityrus sing*. Ronsard is referring to the first of the *Eclogues*, in which two fictional characters, Tityrus and Meliboeus, converse. The conversation has to do both with the beauty of the Mantuan countryside and with the pain of exile. The theme of exile is strong through the poem, and appears again in Ronsard's line 41, which echoes the opening of Psalm 137, "By the waters of Babylon we sat down and wept."

Lines 40–41. *Alexandre le blond* (light haired Alexander) is Ronsard's translation of Homer's title for Paris, ξανθὸς Ἀλέξανδρος.

Line 49 and following. This section of the poem has many close relatives and ancestors. Virgil's *Georgics* are present throughout the poem. Laumonier mentions also Peletier's *Automne* (1547), Belleau's *Vendangeurs*, de Baif's *Vie des champs*. These correspondences should not obscure Ronsard's purposes in the composition of this poem. There is, first, in its construction, the comparison between the grim harvest happening at the time of writing in Paris (Autumn in the first two lines being assigned the verb *moissoner*, is imagined as if it (or he) were laying corpses out, like hay, or wheat); and the grape harvest. There was also the purpose, common to the *Brigade*, of making the real world, the actual language and countryside, serve as the subject of important poetry. This grape harvest is described in terms that have technical and sociological accuracy. The accuracy in itself indicates that Ronsard's interest is as much encyclopedic as it is "poetic" in the selfish way that implies solipsism. The different tasks described were performed as distinctly defined and limited labors, and were paid according to varying scales. All workers were paid by the day, and received their food as well. The *gacheurs* or *fouleurs* were those who trampled the grapes down in the vat before it went to the *pressoir*. The *coupeurs* cut the grapes. The *hotteurs* carried the cut grapes in baskets to the horse- or ox-drawn carts. (Ronsard has them carry their baskets to the press itself.) A number of men were required to turn the wheel (sometimes instead a simple transverse bar) that worked the press. Ronsard's *mui* (line 65) is the *muid,* a unit of liquid measure. Newly pressed wine was put in barrels of a *queue*, a *muid*, a *demi-queue*, or a *caque* in size. The *muid,* 2.68 hectolitres, is close in size to the hogshead, which measures 52½ imp. gallons. Information for this note is drawn from Yvonne Bezard, *La Vie Rurale dans le sud de la région Parisienne de 1450 à 1560*, Thèse pour le Doctorat ès Lettres présentée a la Faculté des Lettres de l'Université de Paris (1929), pp. 151–155.

Line 59 and following. The marc is what remains after the must (or new wine) has been extracted by foot. That marc, in turn, can be pressed to extract wines of inferior quality.

Having been through the press, the marc is still useful. It is given as fodder to pigs, pigeons, or chickens. It is dried so that its seeds can be removed to fatten horses, or it is used as compost. Or it can be mixed with water and used for the production of an inferior wine suitable for servants and laborers. This information is drawn from the incomparably useful book of Olivier de Serres, *Le Theatre d'Agriculture* . . . , pp. 211–223.

Line 65. *Libra* is the constellation in whose house the sun visits during late September, when the grapes were gathered. She is represented as holding a set of scales.

15. EPITAFE DE FRANÇOIS RABELAIS
Bocage (1554)
L. VI, 20

This burlesque epitaph imitates and commemorates Rabelais. Ronsard's familiarity with Rabelais's work does not seem to have been excessive; nor does it seem likely that the possibility of their meeting should be relied on. I think this poem represents an act of (perhaps left-handed) homage and an opportunity for Ronsard to broaden the spirit that had inspired his *Livret de folastries*, into mythological burlesque, as practiced by Rabelais. (The same burlesque is also evident in *La Grenouille*, in the mythologizing of the ancestral frogs; 19 in this selection.)

Lines 1–6. The biology current in Ronsard's time supposed that corruption was actually a principle of generation. Lice, for instance, were born of the breaking down of tissue between the skin and the flesh. Both corruption and generation are large concepts that cannot be translated into single words. The first line suggests the decomposition, rotting, of the dead body. Corruption here carries the sense of the physical sag and disintegration of flesh. Corruption can mean otherwise simply the breaking down of material form during matter's passage (not necessarily hideous) between one form and the next. If it is an unnecessary, and perhaps insincere, fiction that the decayed body might reappear as a grapevine, it is nevertheless a necessary and honorable member of Ronsard's battery of notions and images that are illustrative of his transformational metaphysics.

Line 11. Ronsard's *Iris*. She is a goddess, is also the rainbow, a messenger of the gods. One of her jobs is to supply the clouds with water with which to rain on the world. The principle of evaporation was well known. (Huguet quotes Nuysement as follows: *L'œil du ciel, attirant la vapeur qui s'esleve, grossit l'air de nuaux, puis coup à coup les creve*.) Iris is a bridge for the transformation of matter—water to vapor to cloud—and a process, similar to "corruption," but prettier.

Line 18. *little dog*. The dog star.

Lines 28–32. Bacchus was the son of Jupiter and Semele. Jupiter had promised Semele, another of his mortal mistresses, that he would grant her any request she might make. Juno, Jupiter's goddess wife, persuaded Semele to ask her lover to manifest himself in his godly appearance for a change. Jupiter sadly obeyed her request, clothed in his proper lightning, and Semele was burned up.

Lines 33–38. References to Rabelais's *Gargantua and Pantagruel*. Ronsard had a faulty title page when he first wrote the poem, which allowed him to think Panurge, instead of Pantagruel, was Gargantua's son. The *Papimanes* are to be found in Book IV, XLVIII. The *Isles of Yesterdays (Les Isles Hieres)*, occur on the title page of the editions of 1546, 1547, and 1553. The *combas d'Episteme* are to be found in Book II, XXX. (These additional notes to Laumonier's are in L. XIX, 74.)

Line 43. *Acheron*. One of the rivers of hell.

Line 45. *sparkling wine*. It has become a tradition to comment on Ronsard's
word *bril*, because nobody is sure what it means. Laumonier's
suggestion that it should mean something that sparkles seems
perfectly fair. Mellerio's suggestion that it could be a phonetic
spelling for *Brie*, the cheese, seems less reasonable. A compromise
suggestion (supposing that compromise were an available alterna-
tive to scholars), might be that the *Brie* misspelled as *bril* could
be the wine of Brie, *"les petits vins blancs de la Brie,"* which
were in liberal supply in Parisian cabarets during the seventeenth
and eighteenth centuries at least, and which presumably existed
earlier (Dion, *Histoire de la vigne* . . . p. 547).

Line 49. *killed*. Ronsard's *cueillis* means *gathered* or *culled*. His poem does
not end with the same sort of surprise, therefore, as does mine.

16. EPITAFE DE JAQUES MERNABLE, JOUEUR DE FARCES
Bocage (1554)
L. VI, 40

This was a translation by Ronsard of a Latin poem by Pontano (1426–
1503). Nothing more is known of Mernable than what this poem tells us.
(L. XIX, 76.)

17. *Cache pour cette nuit ta corne, bonne Lune*
Bocage (1554)
L. VI, 54

A literal translation here will make it easier to explain the kind of
change I have felt it helpful to make, and allow me to explain the kind of
thinking that has caused a change in appearance in the versions of some of
the other sonnets in this selection.

Hide for this night your horn, Good Moon,
That Endymion be always your lover
And without waking sleep on your breast:
That no enchanter ever swerve (or interrupt) you.
Day is hateful to me, night is convenient,
I fear by day the sentry of a near enemy,
By night, braver, I cross among
The camp of spies, protected by the dusk.
You know, Moon, what amorous poison can do,

The God Pan, for the price of a white fleece,
Was able to flex your heart well, and you, distinguished Stars,
Foster the fire that keeps me alight.
For if you will remember, most of you, Constellations,
Would not see yourselves burning in the sky except for having loved.

Ronsard begins by addressing the moon directly, and asking a favor. Apostrophe is a rhetorical short cut that poets gave up centuries after they should have, and it does not seem to be time yet to revive the practice. Therefore the business of speaking directly to the moon has been put off until the beginning of the third stanza (*your* heart), and is assumed rather than openly practiced.

The moon's horns, like those Moses wore coming down from the mountain, were simply rays of light. Ronsard makes a transition, without revealing the machinery that allows that transition, between the moon seen as a round pale light that sends out rays, and a moon that looks like a woman, since it has a "*sein*" and a male human lover, Endymion. Ronsard assumed that the moon could be seen simultaneously as the moon and as the goddess Diana. I have made a transition whose machinery, though still invisible (a suppressed *are*) is more definite. (Horns *are* breasts since they are jammed against each other).

Ronsard could assume that his learned reader would know, what I have to look up to find out, not only that Endymion was a mortal whom Diana took as a lover but further that Jupiter had given him the gift that he might always sleep as much as he wished. Ronsard has merged these traditions with the theme of the *aubade*, into something that intends to mean roughly: Moon, cover your light so that it will be dark forever; then Endymion, who gets to sleep as much as he wants, won't be awakened, and you can sleep with him. Furthermore since you will have become invisible, magicians can't find you and force you to change your course (i.e., leave the mountain, Latmos, where you are sleeping with him), as the credulous believed still to be possible in the sixteenth century.

My version attempts to include this background by forcing in the word *darkness*, to make the situation clear. My first stanza is obscure, but is expected to present a strong enough cluster of ideas that some sense will necessarily hover around them.

Ronsard's second quatrain elaborates on the advisability of maintaining the night, and in doing so calls upon the services of the reader's expected familiarity with the contradictories of the Petrarchan love sonnet. It also makes another secret transition. What had been Endymion's place in the first quatrain is now occupied by Ronsard who under cover of darkness slips into what has taken the moon's place, the "camp of spies" or enemy neighbor. That enemy is none other than the sweet (female) enemy who fills the songs of courtly love.

Now, finally (first tercet) once he has gained the safety of the enemy camp, Ronsard continues his request of the moon, man to man, as if the moon and he have had similar experience. "Your heart was bent and pierced, etc." is a *petitio ad hominem*—You should do this for me, Moon (that is, hide your light), since you've been through the same trouble as I have. That experience of the moon's has to do with the supposed fable that Pan (whom I call the Goat God in order that he be more visible) offered Diana the pick of his herd, and then changed himself into a fine white ram, which Diana chose to be her gift; and which proceeded to take advantage of her. My line "The Goat God took you in on a white sheep skin" is deliberately more sexual in its implication, in order that the nature of the submerged story can come across. In Ronsard's eleventh line it becomes clear that he is making two simultaneous requests in the poem. One: Moon, hide your light (for all the reasons that are now clear); and, Stars, foster the fire etc. Under Ronsard's formal grammatical sequence, it is just possible to retain enough memory of the initial imperative (*Lune, cache . . .*) to realize that this is a parallel construction when the second (*Astres, favorisés . . .*) arrives. I don't expect that parallel to be a necessary part of the rhetorical construction. It necessitates, for one thing, another apostrophe, to match the first one which I have already suppressed in my version. What does seem important is that Ronsard is claiming a kinship first with the moon, and then with the stars. The fire that keeps him alight (Ronsard's line 12) is love, which is regarded as a physical principle of the Cosmos, as well as something one person feels for another. We have already seen Hercules become a flaming constellation (11) and there are other examples—the Pleiades, Calisto, Andromeda, Ariadne— whom Ronsard can refer to. The stars are expected to favor Ronsard because they, like him, are maintained by love.

For Ronsard, and for enough of his contemporaries, the constellations are deemed to be important and effective bodies. Our sense of that power is lost. I am imagining that our term "deep space," though obviously completely out of reach of Ronsard's version of the universe, is a term numinous enough to convey to the twentieth-century reader something of the majesty that Ronsard intends to imply.

18. *Cesse tes pleurs, mon livre, il n'est pas ordonné*
Bocage (1554)
L. VI, 56

Here again a literal translation will show the differences between my version and the rhetorical structure within which Ronsard was working.

Cease your tears, my book. It is not ordained
By destiny, that, I living, you get your glory:
Before I have passed beyond the black shore,
The honor that they owe you will not be given you.

After a thousand years I see that somebody amazed
Will come from far away to drink my Loir out of my verses,
And seeing my country, barely be willing to believe
Such a poet was born in so small a field.

Take, my book, take heart. The precious skill
Of a man while he lives is always hateful:
But after he is dead everyone thinks him a god.

Rancor always harms those who are alive.
Over the skills of a dead man, it has no purchase,
And posterity gives honor without envy.

Ronsard changed portions of this poem frequently, right up until the last edition over which he presided, that of 1584. His emendations do not always improve the poem, and I have thought it best to reprint the text in its earliest form. However, it may withdraw some confusion about my version if I indicate some of the Ronsard variants that have influenced my reading.

Lines 3–4. 78–87 *Avant que l'homme passe outre la rive noire, L'honneur de son travail ne luy est pas donné*

Liunes 5–6. 60–87 *Quelcun apres mile ans de mes vers estonné Viendra (84–87 Voudra) dedans mon Loir comme en Pegasse (67–87 Permesse) boire*
Pegasse, or *Permesse*, is the same spring as Pope's Pierian spring, and the source of my "magic water." Ronsard is drawing the contrast between the river Styx (*la rive noire*) and the river Loir, which he has made sacred to the Muses.

Lines 8. 78 *Ronsard se vante né*

19. LA GRENOUILLE A REMY BELLEAU DU PERCHE
Bocage (1554)
L. VI, 83

This is one of a group of animal poems that were included in the *Bocage*. It is of a type called *Blason*, a humorous, satirical, rather pompous expansion of the trivial. I have removed a large part of this poem. Ronsard himself, in the edition of 1578, cut out the final fifty-two lines. I have cut lines 73–110 only, leaving the final two stanzas. What has been removed is the burlesque legend of the frogs' warning to the gods, which was the reason for the reward of a brief life. To have included that story here would have seriously weakened the effect of the same story when it appears in *The Hymn to the Stars* (25), and asks to be taken seriously.

Laumonier's notes give a good deal of information about the sources (principally Pliny's *Natural History*) for the material the poem presents. I will not repeat that, but merely add to it.

Line 18. *greek*. Ronsard's *coaçer* recalls the chant from Aristophanes' *The Frogs*.

Line 50. Laumonier finds reference to the medical use of the frog's heart, and its eyes. I will add to that the description from the *Jardin de Santé* of the uses to which the frog, and its parts, can be put.

On dit que le gisier de la raine est double. Aussi si les raines sont bruslees vives en ung vaisseau de terre la cendre dicelles mise avec miel fait venir les cheveulx au lieu dont ils sont cheuz & encores font la chose mieulx quant elle est mise avec poix liquide. On dit que la brouet de la raine cuyte en une paesle guerist la toux. Le fiel des raines oste les vers qui naissent en l'homme. Et proffite la cendre du fiel des raines contre fievres. . . . (f. xi, verso, *Des Bestes*).

(They say that the frog's gizzard is double. Also, that if frogs are broiled alive in an earthen vessel, the ashes mixed with honey will cause hair to return to the places whence it has fallen; and will do that job still better when it is mixed with liquid pitch. They say that the broth of a frog, cooked in a frying-pan, heals the cough. The bile of frogs brings out the worms that engender in people. And the ashes of the bile are useful against fevers. . . .)

Line 86. The toad has long been considered poisonous. Since the toad was imagined to be generated out of mud or, in some cases, from decayed vegetable matter—Fayol goes so far as to say that the eggs of ducks can be converted in such a way as to generate toads (*L'Harmonie Celeste . . .* p. 346–347), the *Hymenée*, which I have translated as "wedding slime," and which I suppose to be the fertilized eggs of the toad, would not have been understood to be potential toads. It is a shame that one as fascinated by metamorphoses as Ronsard was, should not have realized the metamorphic processes that could have been seen among the batrachians.

20. ODE A JACQUES DE RUBAMPRÉ
Meslanges (1555)
L. VI, 195

This is one of the Odes that Ronsard felt to be imitative of Anacreon.

Line 8. *Rhadamanthus.* The son of Jupiter and Europa. He became one of the judges of hell, and forced the dead to confess their crimes.

21. ODELETTE A L'ARONDELLE
Meslanges (1555)
L. VI, 230

Line 12. Ronsard's line says, of course, "My Cassandra from between my arms."

22. ODELETTE (*La terre les eaux va boivant*)
Meslanges (1555)
L. VI, 256

This is directly modeled on *Anacreonta*, 22.

23. ODE A SA MAITRESSE
Meslanges (1555)
L. VI, 258

24. ODE (*Ma douce jouvance est passée*)
Les quatre premiers livres des Odes (1555), XVIII
L. VII, 102

25. HYMNE DES ASTRES A MELIN DE SAINCT GELAIS
Les Hymnes (1555)
L. VIII, 150

    In 1555 and 1556 Ronsard published a number of hymns on various subjects in alexandrine couplets which he called *"vers heroiques,"* and we call "heroic couplets."

    The heroic couplet is beautifully adapted to the expression of irony (as Pope, in English, uses it), or to the expression of statements about which it is expected there will be no argument.

    Ronsard used the hymn form as the vehicle for a presentation of a large body of encyclopedically collected information and, I think, as a sort of first attempt at the epic form.

    Ronsard had models to follow in the so-called Homeric hymns; in the works of Callimachus, Lucretius; in the Vergilian epic; in all of which, to varying degrees, information and a responsibly rational piety were knit together in a form that was graceful, ponderous, and moved as inevitably as a juggernaut.

    While this group of hymns, coming from Ronsard's hand, may seem to us surprisingly sententious—we are better prepared for the subtler, more mercurial shifts in tone in the later hymns to the four seasons—I think the tone consistent with what I believe to have been Ronsard's intention: the collection and preservation of a body of wisdom for his own, and future, generations.

At the same time, the hymns retain an intimate quite personal quality. The way in which the attraction between the poet and the person to whom the poem is dedicated is kept track of, serves as a structural principle. In the *Hymn to the Stars*, for instance, when the name of Melin surfaces again in line 164, we realize that the poem has been carefully brought back into his presence, and is working almost conversationally.

The other hymns have as their subjects Death, Gold, Heaven, Philosophy, Justice, Eternity, the Daimons.

For further study of the Hymns, see Laumonier's introduction to the eighth volume of the series; Albert-Marie Schmidt, *Hymne des Daimons* édition critique et commentaire (Paris, 1939); Germaine Lafeuille, *Cinq Hymnes de Ronsard* (Geneva, 1973).

Line 1. *Melin* de Saint-Gelais, a court poet of considerable influence, with whom Ronsard had concluded a feud. This poem was intended to reestablish their relationship. Saint-Gelais had published some ten years previously *Advertissement sur les jugements d'astrologie*, and a *Chanson des Astres*.

Line 7. *firmament*. In Genesis the firmament is an inverted bowl that keeps the heavenly waters from falling on, and mixing again with, the earthly waters from which they were separated. Ronsard's firmament is that described in the eleventh century by Honoré d'Autun, *"Le ciel supérieur se nomme firmament, parce qu'il a été consolidé au milieu des eaux. Il est de forme sphérique, de nature aqueuse, orné partout d'étoiles. Il a été formé aux dépens de ces eaux par une consolidation qui l'a rendu semblable à la glace ou mieux encore au cristal."* (cited by Lafeuille, *Cinq Hymnes* . . . p. 24). (The superior sky is named the firmament, because it has been consolidated in the midst of the waters. It is spherical in form, of a watery nature, decorated throughout with stars. It was made up at the expense of (which means, probably, simply "out of the material of") these waters by a solidification that made it similar to ice or, more accurately, crystal.)

Ronsard's lines, added in 1587 to the *Hymne du Ciel* (and cited also by Lafeuille, p. 23) demonstrate more clearly his adherence to this bit of cosmology:

> Tes murs sont de crystal et de glace espoissie
> Des rayons du Soleil fermement endurcie,
> Où tes feux sont clouez, ainçois tes grands flambeaux.

(Your walls are of crystal and thick ice
Firmly hardened by the rays of the sun,
Where your fires are nailed, like your great torches.)

The "hard heaven's edge" (my line 6) is justified, therefore, by Ronsard's understanding of the word *firmament*.

Line 9. *guilty*. Ronsard's *coupable* does not really intend to assign moral responsibility to the stars' influence—nor, exactly, a legal one. But the responsibility is there, and Ronsard cannot overemphasize it.

Lines 10, 11. Ronsard is punning on the name *Melin*, supposing it to relate to the word *miel* (honey), and the plant *Melissa* (lemon balm), which, like thyme, bees were reputed to favor.

Line 66. These are the so-called fixed stars.

Line 79. *our souls are free.* Ronsard is struggling to maintain the required element of the freedom of the human will.

Line 90. *Tiphys* was the pilot of Jason's ship the Argo, during the expedition to Colchis.

Line 99. My "with a straight, tight line," which suggests the means by which rows could be made straight, may be an unwarranted conclusion from Ronsard's *"d'une droite ligne,"* "in straight rows."

Line 102. *grafted* might be more properly put as *layered*.

Lines 157–162. This is the doctrine of the humors. The stars, and the moon and planets, have their own individual temperaments (Saturn, cold and dry; Jupiter, hot and humid; Mars, cold and dry; Venus, hot and humid, etc.). And their celestial dispositions have continual effect on the balance of the four humors within the human body: the balance (or imbalance) of those humors determining human temperaments. The Astral accompaniment to one's birth determines one's prevailing temperament, which will then vary according to the astral arrangements of the moment. Fayol (*L'Harmonie Celeste* . . .) discusses all this in great detail, since it is the ultimate purpose of his book to prepare for a description of the way in which the stars' influence over plants and animals makes them work as healing agents for human infirmities, which the stars themselves either cause, or exacerbate.

Line 163. *marked boundaries.* Ronsard's *"bornes"* I guess to be the signs of the zodiac.

Line 167. *whole cities* . . . The time of a city's foundation was supposed to assign it a prevailing astrological influence and, as it were, temperament.

Lines 192–200. Ronsard denies the possibility that the stars could be nourished on the earth's liquids, first, by the chemical argument that since they are fire, they would be "corrupted," i.e., put out, by water, which is antithetical to fire; second that, if they are to be eternal, they must nourish themselves, on their own fire. (Something that depends on exterior nourishment must be corruptible.)

26. ODELETTE (*Les espics sont à Cerés*)
Les quatre premiers livres des Odes (1555)
L. VII, 105

27. *Le vingtiesme d'Avril couché sur l'herbelette*
Continuation des Amours (1555) XVII
L. VII, 134

Text of 1578

> This dream, or vision, recalls Petrarch's Sonnet CXC, *Una candida cerva*. It is an allegorical presentation of the moment of encounter when the poet falls in love with his beloved (who, by this point in Ronsard's development, is being called Marie).

28. *Marie, levez-vous, ma jeune paresseuse*
(*Mignongne, levées-vous, vous estes paresseuse*)
Continuation des Amours (1555)
L. VII, 140

Text of 1578

29. *J'ay desiré cent fois me transformer, et d'estre*
Continuation des Amours (1555), XLV
L. VII, 162

Text of 1578

Literally:

> A hundred times, I have wanted to transform myself, and be
> An invisible spirit, in order to hide myself
> At the bottom of your heart, so as to investigate the humor
> That makes you appear so cruel against me.

> If I were inside you, at least I would be master
> Of the humor that makes you sin against love;
> And so you would have neither pulse, nor nerves beneath the flesh,
> That I might not search out in order to understand you.

> I would know, in spite of you and your tendencies,
> All of your intentions, and your states,
> And I would chase so well the coldness from your veins
>
> That the flames of love would ignite you there:
> Then when I saw them all filled with his fire
> I would make myself a man again, and then you would love me.

Ronsard's poem depends upon familiarity with, and acceptance of, the chemico-psychological system of the humors (over which the stars have already been seen to have some control [25]). I have suppressed the system of the humors from my version. The word *humor* that appears in line three is really nothing more than our vestigial remnant of that system, and means, rather vaguely, *mood*. Ronsard's primary interest is not in the mechanical system of invasion, but in the invasion itself, its purpose and its desired result. This is a case where it seemed to me that his intention would best be served by my concealing his machinery.

30. *Vous mesprisez nature: estes vous si cruelle* (*Hé que voulez vous dire? estes vous si cruelle*) Nouvelle Continuation des Amours (1556) **L. VII, 254**

Text of 1578

This may be one of the best examples of the style (the so-called *style bas*, or low style) which Ronsard is developing during this period. He has been anxious to remove pretensions, particularly the heavier classical references, from the sonnets; to develop a language that is both graceful and closer to normal conversation; and to rely more and more on the references at hand in the real world around him. This approach forces an increasing intensity to inform the descriptive language; it also begins to open the way for the kind of poetry in which Ronsard, as an older poet, excelled: the description, accurate and polite, of intimate emotional conditions. The foundation in the inherited literature of the Greeks and Romans always remains firm; but it is accepted more casually, and used less as a means of showing off.

I want to mention, in association with this poem, something which I think important to the general appreciation of Ronsard's writing, particularly about nature. It is true that the Renaissance as we think of it brought back into the consciousness of civilized people, books that had long been lost or disregarded. And so Pliny and Cicero and Hesiod came into the courts, libraries, and colleges again. But in the meantime, during what the enlightened later called the Dark Ages, there was a continuous strain of habit, custom, usage, that linked the ancient civilizations to the medieval, and through those dark ages had remained constant enough that the world described by Vergil was still in very important ways the world that Ronsard actually saw. People remembered the names of plants, and what they were good for, even after they had forgotten their Pliny, and without reading Averoës. The customs of farming—and it was farming that conquered Europe much more effectively than legions—remained constant. It is the memory as well as the actual practice of Roman farming, that Ronsard saw around him. Since Ronsard knew his Vergil well it is not surprising that when he speaks of the countryside he frequently says what Vergil has said in the *Georgics* already. But we must remember also that Ronsard saw farmers doing many of the things that Vergil had told them to do fifteen hundred years earlier; and Hesiod had told them to do still earlier.

It is difficult for us, who are hemmed in by tractors, to appreciate the immediacy, the currency, of images which to us have become jaded, embarrassing, and meaningless. An example: Ronsard's *"la jeune vigne embrasse les ormeaux,"* we understand immediately, out of habit, and because of its context, to be mildly and pleasantly sexual. (The young vine hugs the elm trees.) But we don't know beyond that what it means. Some research into Renaissance imagery gives us the additional knowledge that it is a common line and a common symbol—Philibert de l'Orme, the architect, represents himself in a picture whose background includes a punning reference to his name—an elm around which a vine is growing: a vine, moreover, with grapes on it. *Le Premier Tome de l'Architecture* (Paris, 1568).

We then become distracted further into literary symbolism, and learn that a clerk in the eleventh century says, "The elms . . . if they bear no fruit, at least offer the sustaining of their trunks to the vine and its grapes; they are symbolic of the great of the world, held, by duty, to the support of the Church and its spiritual works (Dion, *Histoire de la vigne* . . . p. 188).

We pursue the image into classical literature and find sources in Vergil. *Georgics* I, 2, "Under what sign . . . one should join the vine to the elm"; II, 221, "That (land) will wrap your elms in happy vines"; and by Book II, 360, we discover that not only is the image repeated but in fact Vergil is instructing his husbandmen in the method by which grapevines are purposely trained to grow up elm trees. So there is a basis in custom for the image.

Further exploration in Pliny leads us to a passage which not only repeats the sexual nature of the image but adds further circumstantial evidence to the currency of the practice: "In the country of Campaine about Capua, they [vines] be set at the roots of poplars, and (as it were) wedded unto them: and so being suffered to wind and clasp about them as their husbands, yea, and with their wanton arms or tendrils to climb aloft, and with their joints to run up their boughs, they reach up to their head, yea, and overtop them: insomuch as the grape-gatherer in time of vintage, putteth in a clause in the covenants of his bargain when he is hired, that in case his foot should fail him, and he break his neck, his master who sets him awork should give order for his funeral fire and tomb at his own proper cost and charges." *Selections from The History of the World,* trans. Philemon Holland, ed. Paul Turner (Arundel, Eng.: Centaur Press Ltd., 1962), p. 145.

It is comforting to find the image so firmly rooted in the practice of the ancients; but we are left with a lingering fear that Ronsard is merely being derivative and "poetic" until we learn that the practice of training the grapevines for height, on trees, was still so common in sixteenth-century France, that de Serres spends much time and eloquence discouraging his countrymen from the practice (de Serres, *Le Theatre d'Agriculture* . . . pp. 153–200.)

Since we have become used to the idea of the grapevine pruned to grow laterally, and never any taller than four feet above the ground, we are unprepared for Ronsard's image—unless by chance we have happened upon the vineyards in Italy, perhaps still in the south of France, where that method of viticulture is still occasionally practiced.

31. CHANSON (*Je veux chanter en ces vers ma tristesse*) (*Je ne veux plus que chanter de tristesse*) Nouvelle Continuation des Amours (1556) L. VII, 277

Text of 1578

This *Chanson* relies on Petrarchan models for its central argument: an illustration of the extent to which an emotional state (being-in-love) affects the mind's ability to make pictures, or to perceive the realness of its surroundings. Petrarch seems to us, from our vantage point, to have initiated the poet's ability to report the world as if it were an extension of himself (i.e., this place is a good image of how sad I feel).

Ronsard's concern is not quite so introverted. The countryside he sees is infected, not by his own image, but by that of another person, "Marie," whom he wishes for so much as to see her in the world around him.

Our psychology has almost completely withdrawn from our repertory the notion of the eye as an active, aggressive, effective organ. The more lively and interesting our visions become, the more likely we are to be told that our "projections" have nothing to do with the real world, and couldn't possibly hurt anybody.

Ronsard is working in a time which still maintains a healthy fear of the evil eye, an organ of malicious intent which operates solely by means of the function of seeing. The eye has some real power to change the world by its operation.

Our word imagination (Ronsard, line 18, uses the word), has come to mean a rather impotent and solipsistic act whose fruit is private in real life although it is sometimes turned into art and shared around. The word has a more powerful origin, much closer to Ronsard's time and thinking than it is to ours, which means not the "making up" but the *casting* of images; the casting of one's own image, or of oneself *as* an image, onto something or someone else.

Jean de Venette, writing in 1348 of the great plague, says "This sickness or pestilence was called an epidemic by the doctors. . . . This plague and disease came from *ymaginatione* or association and contagion, for if a well man visited the sick he only rarely evaded the risk of death." *The Chronicle of Jean de Venette*, trans. Jean Birdsall (New York, 1953), p. 49.

In doing my version I have been particularly concerned to keep clear the relation between the poet's "imagining" and the scenes he describes. My swervings from Ronsard's text in this case will have to do either with a modernizing, and shortening, of Ronsard's logical structure; or with making his images more visible to the modern reader. In one case (Ronsard's lines 25–28), I have substituted one image for another, thinking that the argument from optics is not as strong today as Ronsard would wish it.

32. ODE (*Dieu vous gard, messagers fidelles*)
Nouvelles Continuation des Amours (1556)
L. VII, 294

Following Ronsard's example (in the editions of 1578–1587), I have suppressed the final stanza. I include it here in order to show the direction of Ronsard's thinking when he first wrote the poem.

> Sus, page, à cheval, que lon bride:
> Ayant ce beau printemps pour guide,
> Je veux ma dame aller trouver,
> Pour voir en ces beau mois si elle
> Envers moy sera moins cruelle
> Qu'elle ne m'a esté l'yver.

> Page, rush to the horse and bridle it:
> Having this beautiful springtime as my guide
> I want to go and find my lady
> To see whether, in these beautiful months, she
> Will be less cruel toward me
> Than she was toward me during the winter.

Ronsard's gradual movement away from mythologizing leads him to develop, more and more, two kinds of theme. One is the nature of his own psychological state (which we have seen described as melancholic in 31—a state that, before Ronsard's time, people normally wished to cure—but which during and after his time some people, particularly poets, found so productive as to warrant cultivation); the other is the value of the real world around him, to which he wishes to be a guide.

Any poem has some curative intention. The very act of undertaking any logical arrangement has to do with correction, or with the reestablishment of balance. In this poem, as first presented, the argument is simple: Spring is doing all this; therefore I'll see if it's done it to my lady, so that I in turn can do it. This spring poem, if read beside another spring poem of a later year (1569), *La Salade* (40), will immediately be seen to be a close relative.

It is clear that spring is prompting a change in mood and in intention. What is not clear is how that comes about. I want, without suggesting that this is some kind of cabalistic coded rigamarole which only the initiated can comprehend, to suggest that there is more careful thinking here than the simple "In the Spring a young man's fancy . . ." rather inane argument. I want to suggest that, just as Ronsard is aware of the medicinal operations of the plants he gathers for his salad in the later poem, he seems to be aware of them here also, in that the plants he chooses to mention (which, incidentally, are not all in flower simultaneously), with the exception of the two whose presence derives from their myths (Narcissus and Hyacinth), have operative values which, when combined, are consistent with the poem's described intention and argument. I will list the plants in order, and put with them those virtues that seem relevant, drawn either from *Le Jardin de Santé* or from Gerard.

Paquerette. Daisy. "The juice of the leaves and roots snift up into the nosthrils purgeth the head mightilie of foule and filthie slimie humours: and helpeth the Megrim." (Gerard)

Rozes. Rose. It is impossible to be certain what particular rose Ronsard intends (if, indeed, it makes any difference). The (unspecified) rose has been so long so common a symbol. While Gerard distinguishes carefully one species from another, *Le Jardin de Santé* makes no such distinction. The rose is, of course, used elsewhere as an exemplum of impermanence. It was widely used both for culinary and medical purposes, and had among its virtues, twice mentioned in the *Jardin de Santé*, the power to "comfort the heart."

fleurettes de Mars. Violets. (March violets.) Gerard, while introducing the flower, says of Violets ". . . Gardens themselves receive by these the greatest ornament of all, chiefest beauty, and most gallant grace; and the recreation of the minde which is taken heereby, cannot be but verie good and honest: for they admonish & stir up a man to that which is comely & honest; for flowers through their beautie, varietie of colour, and exquisite forme, do bring to a liberall and gentle manly minde, the remembraunce of honestie, comelinesse, and all kinds of vertues." Gerard mentions further "The latter phisitions do think it good to mix drie Violets with medicines, that are to comfort and strengthen the hart."

Thyn. Thyme. Gerard: ". . . is profitable also for such as are fearfull, melancholike, and troubled in minde. . . . Of his native propertie it releeveth them which be melancholike. . . ."

Anise. Anise. Gerard: "stirreth up bodily lust." *Le Jardin de Santé*: ". . . *augmente et croist le laict aux femmes et le sperme et semence aux hommes . . .*" (augments and increases milk in women, and the sperm and seed in men), "*Et si esmeut et aguillone le vouloir de habiter charnellement et augmente le sperme.*" (And it moves and goads the desire to have intercourse; and augments the sperm.) "*Anis aussi incite a luxure et libidinite, et quant la fumigation de sa vapeur est odores, il oste et guerist la douleur de la teste.*" (Anise also incites luxury and lechery, and when the fumigation of its vapor is smelled, it removes and cures headache.)

235

Melisse. Lemon Balm (Bawme). *Le Jardin de Santé: "Et de sa propriete est a ayder a la debilite du cueur, et oste la cardiaque passion. Et si oste les afflictions, solicitudes et esbahissements qui adviennent de melencolie. . . ."* (And among its properties is that it aids the debility of the heart, and relieves heart-suffering. And it relieves the afflictions, anxieties, and upsets that come from melancholy.)

33. A SON LIVRE
Nouvelle Continuation des Amours (1556)
L. VII, 315

Text of 1578

This long poem (200 lines), from which I have removed the beginning and the end, Ronsard used first as the epilogue for his *Nouvelle Continuation des Amours,* and later as the introduction to the *Second Livre des Amours.* It is a curious poem, formal, defensive, intimate, jocular, bitter in tone, by turns. Through a series of jokes and stories Ronsard passes from a mock defense of having a series of lovers (in which he also pokes fun at his model, Petrarch, for staying constant so long to a single woman, and she unresponsive), to the main purpose of the poem: his announcement that he feels that his new style, pleasant and unpretentious, is adapted to speaking the truth either to a single lover, or to those of us who are *"de nature amiables."*

Ronsard's final line would be translated literally: "And who, till death, will not be fickle (or changeable)." I believe that he is approaching his readers directly here, and with an intimacy that recalls the relationship between himself and his book at the poem's opening.

In my version I have left out the tiger reference, Ronsard's lines 22–25.

34. *D'un sang froid, noir, et lent, je sens glacer mon cœur*
Second livre des Meslanges (1559)
L. X, 90

35. *Marie, baisez moy: non: ne me baisez pas*
(Sinope, baisez moy . . .)
Second livre des Meslanges (1559)
L. X, 96

Text of 1578

36. LE VOYAGE DE TOURS, OU LES AMOUREUS THOINET ET PERROT
Le Second Livre des Amours (1560)
L. X, 214

Text of 1578

I have cut from Ronsard's text in order to reduce the bulk of this poem, lines 48–56, 81–126, 141–162, 173–180, 275–280, 301, 302. The poem is carefully balanced, and its form depends on the repetition and reflection of sentiments between the speeches of Thoinet and Perrot. I would hope that the reader who is attracted to the poem in its present form, will read it in its entirety.

This is a delicate poem, which plays with the themes of courtly love, and of the shepherd-and-shepherdess routines; but is playful without ever being really burlesque. It is Ronsard's most successful comedy, and some of his most luxuriant love poetry.

Thoinet is Antoine de Baïf, a fellow member of the *Brigade*. *Perrot* is Ronsard himself. *Phellipot* is Philippe de Ronsard, Pierre's older brother.

It is a fair presumption that the poem depends for its principal structure on a real journey which has been embroidered upon, both in the journeying, and in the remembering.

The bulk of my notes to this poem will have to do with the medical, even magical, properties of the plants mentioned. But that fact should not distract the reader into assuming that this plant lore is more than a secondary interest to the poet.

Line 1.   *Flora,* the goddess of flowers, is the wife of *Zephyrus,* the west wind.

Line 11.   The action takes place in the Loire (and the Loir) valley; begins at Ronsard's birthplace near Coutures-sur-Loir; passes to the island in the Loire on which was situated the priory of Saint-Cosme, whose prior Ronsard was to become (he was eventually buried there); and ends in the city of Tours.

Line 45.   *drift ice.* Ronsard says, literally: I found your chest and ear full, Alas! who would have thought it? with a hundred thousand (pieces of) ice, which did not permit you to hear my songs.

Line 51.   *the black wave,* the water of Lethe, one of the rivers of Hell, which eradicates memory.

Lines 63–64.   In Ronsard's lines 81–126, Thoinet tells of having tried different forms of magic to learn what the outcome of his love for Francine will be. He first consults a witch; then tries a form of divination still practiced, according to Laumonier, in Vendomois and its surroundings, which is done with the *"joncq,"* or *Armoise vulgaire,* cut on the eve of the feast of Saint John. This plant is also known as *Artemisia mater Herbarum,* (Artemisia, the herb mother) because, as the *Jardin de Santé* has it, *elle est medicine privee et convenable a toutes les maladies et maulx des femmes* (it is medicine proper and suitable to all female illnesses and sickness). Gerard, who calls the same plant by the less romantic name of Mugwoort, says of it (after noting its applicability to infirmities associated with the female generative organs), "Many other fantasticall devices invented by Poets are to be seene in the workes of the auncient writers, tending to witchcraft and sorcerie, and the great dishonor of God: wherefore I do of purpose omit them as things unworthie of my recording or your reviewing."

We use it to flavor vermouth.

Artemisia, in sum, is a plant whose medical and magical properties coincide; and is, further, cited by Ronsard on account of those properties.

When divination by *Armoise* fails to produce the desired answer, Thoinet tries another form, using the leaves of the *coudrier,* the hazel. The hazel is best known now for its use in the divination of water (dowsing); The use to which it is put here is simple and magical: Thoinet holds the leaves in his hand, agitates them, and fails to produce the crackling sound that would indicate the fire of love burning in his Francine's heart. Laumonier mentions in his notes that the wood is thought to have magical properties, and that the *"baguette des fées,"* or fairy wreath, is still made from it. It is upon a hazel tree that *Perrot* will place a wreath of flowers later in this poem.

Line 82. *Thyme.* (See n. 32).

> *lily of the valley.* (Muguet). According to both Gerard and the *Jardin de Santé,* it "comforts" the heart. It does in fact contain a heart stimulant.

> *Cassandra* (Cassandrette). A note by Belleau says that a red flower, commonly called *gantelée,* has been given the name Cassandra by Ronsard. I am unable to identify this flower, or that *"fleur de Nostredame"* which Du Bellay rechristened *Olivette.* Baïfs *Francine* is given as a name, by him, to the Anemone, which as late as 1907 (R. C. Wren, *Potter's New Cyclopaedia of Medicinal Herbs and Preparations*) was recommended as "much esteemed as a remedy for nerve exhaustion in women, especially when due to menstrual troubles."

Line 127. *Hesper.* Esacus, son of Priam, was changed to a diver (or loon) on account of his love for Hesper.

Line 153. *Glaucus.* A sea god, who was represented as a merman. He had been a fisherman and had noticed that the fish he caught, when he dropped them in the grass, jumped about vigorously and escaped into the water again. Thinking that their energy must come from the grass itself, he ate some, and escaped into the water himself, where his shape was suitably transformed.

Lines 170–174. *Periwinkle.* (*parvenche*) Gerard ". . . stoppeth the inordinate course of the monethly sicknesse."

Thyme. (See n. 32)

lavender. (*aspic porte-epy, la grande lavande*) Gerard's "Lavander spike," ". . . doth helpe the panting and passion of the hart."

pennyroyal. (*poliot*) Gerard's Pennie royall, or Pudding grasse; in Latin, *pulegium*; in French, *Pouliot*. It ". . . provoketh the monethly termes, bringeth foorth the secondine, the dead childe and unnaturall birth . . ." Jean Maveric, *La Médecine Hermétique des Plantes* (Paris, 1917), p. 33, lists it with *armoise* and *thyn* as effective for troubles of the matrix.

water lily. (*neufard, nenuphar: Nymphea*) This has a confusing reputation, which makes it a tricky addition to the assemblage. Rabelais mentions the water lily *Nymphaea heraclea* as being the enemy of lecherous monks (Book III, chapter 50). The *Jardin de Santé* cites it for its (perfectly fitting) soporific properties; but gives to its root as well, when drunk with syrup of poppy, the power to remove the desire for "luxury," and to congeal the sperm. These properties are already the poppy's alone (the effects of opium are well known). Given the circumstances of the poem, it seems the roots would be well avoided. The flowers, according to Gerard, "being made into oile, as yee de make oile of roses, doth coole & refrigerate, causing sweat and quiet sleepe, and putting away all venereous dreames: the temples of the head & palmes of the hands and feete, and the brest being anointed for the one, and the genitors upon and about them for the other." Since Ronsard specifically mentions the cooling nature of the waterlily (*qui la froideur incite*), it must be this power to produce sweet and quiet sleep that is of interest to him.

rushes. (*jonc qui les bords des rivieres habite*) Le Jardin de Santé assigns the rush pleasantly uncomplicated soporific powers: "*fait dormir et avoir sommeil.*"

Line 133. *Turnus,* the founder of the city of Tours, was supposed to be buried beneath the city's castle, according to Belleau's note.

37. RESPONSE DE P. DE RONSARD, GENTILHOMME VANDOMOIS, AUX INJURES & CALOMNIES DE JE NE SCAY QUELS PRÉDICANS & MINISTRES DE GENEVE, 1563
L. XI, 116

Excerpt, lines 507–564

This poem is a self-defense, written in response to numerous anonymous pamphlets, in which Protestants attacked Ronsard on a number of grounds.

Lines 45–48. In the editions of 1578 and after, these lines were cut out, presumably because they were misread in such a way as not to withdraw credence from the charge of lechery.

38. DISCOURS AMOUREUX DE GENEVRE
Recueil des Nouvelles Poësies (1564)
L. XII, 256

Text of 1578

Excerpt, lines 1–30

The entire poem is 488 lines long and is surprisingly intimate, direct, and straightforward. The section I have translated should be taken as bait, rather than as a complete poem. I have pretended to complete it in my version by adding the partial last line, "Danced for you . . ."

39. LE CHAT, AU SEIGNEUR DE BELLEAU
Sixiesme livre des Poëmes (1569)
L. XV-1, 39

This poem is based on the cosmologies described in notes 9, 10, 11, 15, 25. It might be understood as a compromise between the hymn and the blason (see 19, *La Grenouille*).

Perhaps the quality that stands out most uncomfortably in this poem, is that Ronsard no longer has the energy nor the desire to joke. He is presenting real autobiography and real belief.

We must keep in mind that what seems credulous and embarrassingly naïve, the belief in divination by dream, and by the action of domestic animals, was for Ronsard and for other conservative thinkers of his day a perfectly respectable last-ditch defense of faith in the rationality of the universe. Under this system all things, whether they be the conjunction of planets or the droppings of birds, are reasonable and explainable.

Line 7. *machine.* In essence, a number of interconnected parts that working together produce a harmonious result. A clock is a machine in the sense Ronsard is thinking of, and a machine that was used frequently by philosophers as an example of the way the universe worked.

Line 19. *quickens.* Ronsard's *"La Mer s'esgaye"* means, I believe, "The sea disperses (itself)," and is a reference to the regular rising and falling of the tides.

Line 21. Ronsard's lines 23-25 mean, "I say the earth, happy part of the world, kind mother, with great fecund nipples, large-breasted . . ." I found the insistence on physical attributes difficult to fit into the exalted tone of the general subject.

Line 24. *metals.* Metals were believed to have their existence according to the same principles as plants and animals. Their powers (in medical terms) had to do with the degree to which they contained the *essences,* which would be distilled from them (hot, cold, wet, dry).

I cannot judge how firm, or how elaborate, was Ronsard's belief in *Hermetic,* or *Spagyric* medicine; but its basic idea, that of the purification of matter by means of separating from it its vital principle (which is the imprint of the *Idée,* or *Esprit, divine*), is assumed here.

Jean Mavéric, *La Médecine Hermétique des Plantes . . .* describes the reasoning behind the extraction of this vital principle (the quintessence). I include it because it seems to explain Ronsard's vision of the world; and because it mirrors so closely his sonnet (53) *Si le grain de fourment . . .*

"All bodies are made of *matter* and of *spirit.* Matter is passive and inert, whereas the Spirit is the principle of vital action *(le principe vital-actif),* the imprint of the divine *Idea,* which is the cause of evolution. It is therefore plain that the power of a mixture is in the Spirit, and that this spirit is much more active when it is delivered from its corporal prison.

All the physical side of the spagyric art is in this separation or extraction. To obtain this spirit in the force of its maximum power, one must elevate it; to elevate it one must ripen *(evolve)* it; and to ripen it, one must break down its body, in the same way that the grain rots in the ground before it can germinate.

Now this rotting is no other than the *evolution of matter* to purify and exalt it . . ." (pp. 5, 6).

Line 34. *regions.* These are the spheres, lower, middle, and upper, of differing consistency according to their distance from the earth, which lie between earth and the firmament. Fayol (*L'Harmonie Celeste* . . . p. 43), says that mountains reach into the middle region.

Line 42. *prophets.* The argument is simple. Plants, animals, men (in fact everything) are built according to the universal principle: therefore any member can speak for it.

Lines 67–69. In 1567 Ronsard had published, to small acclaim, the first part of his projected epic, the *Françiade.* A long illness in 1568 kept him in the country and away from court. It seems to be that illness that is referred to in this poem, and in *La Salade* (40).

Line 70. *Demon.* Ronsard's *Hymne des Daimons,* édition critique et commentaire, by Albert-Marie Schmidt (Paris, 1939), gives a great deal more background on Ronsard's understanding of and belief in *"daimons"* than it is necessary to go into here. The *daimon* is a relic of Plato's *Timaeus,* mixed with bits of eastern mythology— and by Ronsard's day is an imagined intermediary between God and created matter who can in some manner participate in matter. This demon is not "the devil" and does not necessarily have any moral value.

Philosophers had called on the *daimonic* element frequently enough, in describing the creation and the behavior of the material world, that the fourth Lateran Council felt it necessary to reaffirm God's immediate responsibility for the creation of everything. *". . . Dieu tout-puissant par sa vertue, ensemblement des le commencement du temps, fit du rien l'une, & l'autre creature, & spirituelle &c . . . a cause de ce decret il falloit tenir pour foy Catholique que les Anges ne furent pas faicts avant ce monde . . ."* Maldonat, *Traicte Des Anges et Demons* . . . pp. 9–15. Maldonat does not hold with Ronsard's *daimons,* but his *demons* (our devils) are part-members of the material world, in that they are nourished on blood, or on cloud-vapor, and are able to have intercourse with humans, in the forms of incubus and succubus. And they are also admitted to have a prophetic power; but it is not proper to their own powers. Rather, when flying around the celestial spheres, they overhear God talking with the angels, and thus know what is going on (Maldonat, p. 164).

Line 76. *malaria.* Ronsard's *fiebvre quart,* or quartan fever, is now known as malaria. Its cause and nature were not known in Ronsard's time.

Line 93. *cat.* The cat was long thought to be venomous, either by the operation of its eyes, or by its fur, according to Fayol, *L'Harmonie Celeste* . . . *p. 292. Le Jardin de Santé* assigns the wickedness of the cat to its habit of carrying its head crooked toward the ground. The cat was also noted for being the familiar of demons.

Line 129. *goose.* Geese were frequently used as watchdogs since they object noisily to all strangers. This is a reference to the goose whose outcry saved the city of Rome.

Line 149. *Aratos's translator.* Belleau had translated Aratos's *Prognostications and Presages.*

40. LA SALADE, A AMADIS JAMYN
Sixiesme livre des Poëmes (1569)
L. XV-1, 76

Amadis Jamyn was Ronsard's secretary and a fellow poet.

In the Middle Ages vegetables were regarded as the food of commoners, those who were not able to afford meat. The salad is the countryman's inheritance. Ronsard is using it here for its reflection of the life away from court.

This poem is a moralizing disquisition on a well-tried subject—the moral inferiority of court life, and a mildly burlesque version of the *reverdie,* or spring song, as practiced by an ill and aging man. I have already suggested (no. 32) the correspondence in motivation between this and other songs in which the vegetation of the spring is put to some use.

Ronsard had been suffering from a recurrence of his malaria. His salad is presumably a joke—but nevertheless an informed joke.

Line 11. *Lamb's lettuce.* (Ronsard's *boursette toffuë*) Its Latin name, in Gerard, is *Lactuca Agnina.* Its modern French name is *mâche,* or *doucette,* or *Valerianelle potagère*; its modern Latin name, *Valerianella olitoria.* Gerard distinguishes between two species, one called Lambes Lettuce, the other Corne sallade; also White potherbe. Aside from mentioning that it makes good salad, Gerard assigns it no particular power. However, it is listed as a febrifuge by Mavéric, *La Médecine Hermétique* . . . p. 26.

Marguerites. (Ronsard's *pasquerette*) Gerard: "The Daisies do mitigate all kinde of paines, but especially of the ioints and goute proceeding from a hot and drie humour . . . the decoction of the fielde Daisie (which is the best for phisickes use) made in water and drunk is good against agues, inflammation of the liver, and all other inward parts."

Line 12. *salad burnet.* (Ronsard's *pimprenelle*) *Le Jardin de Santé "pimpinelle . . . purge le foye et les reins."* Gerard, "Burnet is a singular good herbe for wounds . . . and commended of a number: it stancheth bleeding, and therefore it was named *Sanguisorba,* as well inwardly taken as outwardly applied. . . . The lesser Burnet is pleasant to be eaten in sallads, in which it is thought to make the hart merrie and glad . . ."

Line 14. *rampion.* (Ronsard's *responsette*) Its modern Latin name, *Campanula Rapunculus*; its modern French name, *Campanule Raiponce.* Gerard lists three Rampions, or Wilde Bell flowers, to which he gives the names *Rapuntium maius, Rapuntium parvum,* and *Rapunculus nemorosus,* or Wood Rampion. The third has the smallest root, but, in Gerard's drawing, most closely resembles the *Campanula Rapunculus.* Gerard says, of all the rampions, that the roots are especially used in salads. He makes also a rather hesitant reference to the possibility that decoctions from the roots are good for inflammations of the mouth and other mouth and throat diseases. Mavéric, p. 28, assigns the *raiponce* to the classification of plants that are "refreshing to the blood." Among the companions of raiponce in this classification are *mâche* (boursette) and *groseiller.*

Line 16. *gooseberry.* (Ronsard's *groiseliers*). *The Jardin de Santé,* which lists the gooseberry as *Vua versa* or *grappe verte,* mentions only the use of the berries themselves, which it calls indigestible. Gerard, who gives the Latin name *Vua Crispa* to the Gooseberrie or Feaberrie bush, mentions that the leaves come out in April or sooner. He says, further, that "The yoong and tender leaves eaten rawe in a sallade, provoketh urine, and driveth foorth stone and gravell." Mavéric, p. 32, includes the *groseille* among the *febrifuges.*

Lines 20–24. The recipe is a playful imitation of the procedures by which simples are made, and a continuation of the preparation for the joke in line 28, in which the made salad is called a *"souv'rain bien"* (sovreign remedy, or cure-all), for the fever from which he is suffering.

Line 80. *colossuses.* Many formal state occasions were elaborately planned and choreograhed as grand parades. A king's entry into a city might be welcomed (supposing the arrival to be well-heralded) by large gilded statues of fitting gods or abstractions situated at the city gates.

Line 109. *Vergil's verses. Georgics* VI, 125.

Line 121. *Crassus* was a Roman general who was killed in the campaign against the Parthians from which he had hoped to win a Roman triumph.

Line 125. *never heard of Rome.* Ronsard couldn't have imagined such a state. His words mean, "without seeing Rome."

Line 126. *Hesiod. Works and Days,* 40 and following. Hesiod claims that "asphodel and mallow" are readily available for the finding and eating. Isidore Silver, *Ronsard and the Hellenic Renaissance in France* (St. Louis, 1961) I, 326–330, discusses the continuity of this influence of Hesiod in Ronsard's thinking.

One final note. Fayol, *L'Harmonie Celeste* . . . p. 195, assigns quartan fever to an excess of the melancholy humor (distinguishing it from other kinds of fever, which have other causes). Ronsard's words *extreme langueur* (line 36), *fol* (line 38), *fureur* (line 40), may be seen as more appropriate when we realize that among the attributes of an excess of the melancholic humor, Mavéric lists, p. 65: Mania, delirium, folly, dementia, *"idée fixe,"* abolition of will, *"langeur,"* despair, hypochondria, nostalgia, discouragement, insatiable desire, depression, disgust with life, suicidal tendencies. The melancholic humor slowed the eliminative functions, thus leading to the retention of urea (Mavéric, p. 65); and gout, from which Ronsard suffered, is a disease that is marked by that retention.

Ronsard makes such a point of his salad because through it he is pleasantly disobeying his doctor's orders. The melancholic temperament and the illnesses that are associated with it is to be tempered by a diet consisting in foods that are by nature hot and humid, since the melancholy temperament is cold and dry. The diet Mavéric would propose: dried fruit, dates, preserves, fried potatos, marmalades, roasted chestnuts, honey, dried prunes, *"pain bis"* (see n. 12, line 41), and white bread. Of the vegetables Ronsard is gathering, gooseberries are cold and dry, rampion is cold, burnet cool and dry, daisies cold and moist, lamb's lettuce cold and moist. Jamyn's objection (line 154) is quite reasonable, that this salad will do his employer no good.

41. ODELETTE
Cependant que ce beau mois dure
Septiesme livre des poëmes (1569)
L. XV-2, 204

Line 5. *mingles*. Ronsard's *"meslant"* suggests the gradual mixing in of gray or white hair.

42. *Comme on voit sur la branche au mois de May la rose*
Oeuvres, Amours, Livre II (1578)
L. XVII-2, 125

This poem is made in celebration of the death of the princess Marie de Clèves, wife of Henri de Condé, and mistress of Henri III. She died in 1574. Ronsard's inclusion of a series of poems *"sur le mort de Marie"* to complete his *Second livre des Amours* makes it certain that he is incorporating his own purposes in these poems, even supposing them to be composed originally at the request of royalty.

43. *Ce premier jour de May, Helene, je vous jure*
Oeuvres, Sonnets pour Helene (1578)
L. XVII-2, 194

Text of 1584

Line 2. *Helen.* The sonnet sequence that this poem introduces was addressed
to Hélène de Fonsèques, a member of the court of the queen
mother, Catherine de Medici. Hélène's last name is also given in
its French version, as Surgères. This poem trades on the coincidence
that was part of Hélène's attraction for Ronsard, of her name with
that of the woman over whom the war of Troy was fought.

Line 5. Ronsard's fifth line (*Par le nouveau* . . .) I have left out of my version,
as this personification of Spring seems to be distracting. The line
means, "By the new Spring, the eldest son of Nature."

As I have also left out the nightingales (*rossignols*), birds so
abused by poets in Ronsard's day and after, that to our ears they
seem mythological, and tainted with the worst sorts of poetry. Eliot
tries to defend their realness by concentrating on their liquid sift-
ings. I believe myself that they can use a rest. But I promise this: if
you are trying to sleep in certain parts of Europe, their night singing
will startle you awake.

44. *Ces longues nuicts d'hyver, où la Lune ocieuse*
Oeuvres, Sonnets pour Helene (1578)
L. XVII-2, 264

Text of 1584

This sonnet, which follows a similar pattern to that of *Cache pour cette
nuit ta corne* (17), might be compared to that poem for an idea of how far the
process of aging has brought Ronsard.

My version has shifted some emphasis, and rearranged some ideas. I
think the essence of the poem, the guilty and unquiet satisfaction with the
fruit of the trick of fantasy, must remain paramount.

45. *Quand vous serez bien vieille, au soir à la chandelle*
Oeuvres, Sonnets pour Hélène (1578)
L. XVII-2, 265

Text of 1584

In the interests of clarity, logic, and appropriateness, I have made
some changes. Ronsard's aged Helen has servants and, as an arthritic old lady,

wakes them by speaking the name of her dead poet. My aged Helen *is* the servant (as it were) and is awakened by the sound Ronsard's name itself has made. Ronsard could not have conceived of being servantless. We, some few of whom are servants, can.

The final line has been so imitated and so frequently translated (it was already of a good age when Ronsard used it), that it is difficult to get its message past the threat of triteness. I have thought it most useful to make the rose real, by means of giving it leaves and stem, and let the reader's memory of the *carpe diem* theme make sense of it.

46. *Mon ame mille fois m'a predit mon dommage*
Oeuvres, Sonnets pour Hélène (1578)
L. XVII-2, 281

Text of 1584

Line 7. *The senses etc.* Ronsard's line means: If it (the body, or its sense of sight) finds itself blinded by the rays of a lovely face.

A literal translation of the tercets:

The body would not languish in amorous care
Unless the soul, and the mind, wished it so.
But the soul gives itself up from the first attack

Counseling, like a queen, the body to do likewise.
In the same way the citizen, betrayed by the soldier,
Gives himself up to his enemies when the city is lost.

My version of *esprit* as "free will" is perhaps excessive; but it is certainly consistent with one of Ronsard's themes in this sonnet, and in this sequence, that his being in love is intentionally his doing.

47. *Au milieu de la guerre, en un siecle sans foy*
Oeuvres, Amours diverses (1578)
L. XVII-2, 318

In 1584 this sonnet was included among the Sonnets for Helen, where it seems to belong, although it refers to a court suit that began in 1568, and Ronsard's first meeting with Hélène was in 1570.

The *Thebaïde* of Ronsard's line 11, which I have translated as "fratricidal war," is a reference to the war between the brothers Eteocles and Polynices, Œdipus's sons.

48. *Ma Dame, je me meurs abandonné d'espoir*
Œuvres, Amours diverses (1578)
L. XVII-2, 329

Literally:

> My lady, I die, abandoned by hope.
> The wound is to the bone; I am not the same
> As I was the other day, so much this last illness
> Breaking through patience, has power over me.
>
> I can not touch, taste, hear, or see.
> I have lost all my senses. I am a pale shadow.
> My body is no more than a tomb. Unhappy is (he) who loves,
> Unhappy who lets himself be deceived by love.
>
> Becomes Achilles to the wounds you have made,
> I am Telephus, and will perish:
> Show me, in your pity, your perfect powers,
>
> And with prompt remedy, deign to succor me.
> If, cruel one, you defeat your servant,
> You will not have the laurel for having killed him.

The story in lines 9–11 is that Telephus, having been wounded by the lance of Achilles, would only be healed by the touch of that weapon.

Ronsard's poem plays on the formal parlance of chivalry, and mingles that with clear description of his psychological state. There is no modern substitute for chivalry, in language or behavior. I have let my version rely on the realization of the theme of wounding and healing.

49. *Voyant par les soudars ma maison saccagee*
Œuvres, Amours diverses (1578)
L. XVII-2, 330

Text of 1584

In my version I have concealed, or made less direct, some of the machinery of Ronsard's logical connections; and have left out or made substitutions for some of the references that seem, now, to intrude on the immediacy of the impression from which Ronsard is working.

50. *Helas! voicy le jour que mon maistre on enterre*
Œuvres, Sonnets pour Hélène (1578)
L. XVII-2, 238

> Charles IX died May 30, 1574, and was interred on the thirteenth of
> July. I have removed some of the more unwieldy classical references and
> formalities.

51. *Je chantois ces Sonets, amoureux d'une Heleine*
Œuvres, Sonnets pour Hélène (1578)
L. XVII-2, 294

52. ELEGIE
Voicy le temps, Candé, qui joyeux nous convie
Œuvres (1578)
L. XVII-2, 380

Excerpt, lines 1–30

> Candé is Hurault, Sieur de la Pitardiere, a friend to whom Ronsard
> also addressed the *Satyre.*

53. *Si le grain de forment ne se pourrist en terre*
Œuvres, Epitaphes (1578)
L. XVII-2, 383

> This sonnet is also concerned with the death of Charles IX. It takes its
> opening argument from *John XII*, 24. (See also n. 39, line 24.)

54. *Vous estes deja vieille, & je le suis aussi*
Œuvres (1587)
L. XVIII-1, 221

55. ELEGIE CONTRE LES BUCHERONS DE LA FOREST DE GASTINE
Œuvres, 1584
L. XVIII-1, 143

Excerpt. Lines 19–68

This poem was written as a protest against the destruction of a large part of the forest of Gastine. (see note 2)

Lines 36–38. The sacred oaks around Jupiter's temple in Dodona, Thessaly, were supposed to have had oracular powers. Gerard, somewhat closer to home, reports of the acorns, which he calls Oke Apples, "being broken in sunder about the time of their withering, do fore-shewe the sequell of the yeere, as the expert Kentish husbandmen have observed by the living things founde in them: as if they finde an Ant, they foretell plentie of graine to insue; if a white worme like a Gentill or Maggot, then they prognosticate murren of beasts and cattle; if a Spider, then (saie they) we shall have a pestilence or some such like sicknes to followe amongst men . . ."

Line 45. *Salemvria's valley.* Tempe is the valley in Thessaly between Olympus and Ossa. The river Salemvria flows in it, which was in ancient times known as the Peneus.

56. DES PERES DE FAMILLE, A MONSIEUR S. BLAISE
L. XVIII-1

We do not know the exact date of the composition of this hymn. It was made by Ronsard to be sung by his neighbors, of the parish of St. Blaise (which was next to Ronsard's priory of Croixval), on the feast of St. Blaise, February 3. It is assigned to his last years, by, among others, Germaine Lafeuille, *Cinq Hymnes de Ronsard . . .* p. 17.

Line 15. *corrupted airs.* Air can be corrupted by comets (which were some-times felt to bring plague), by planetary conjunctions. Our word infected means something like what Ronsard is thinking. I find the word corrupt applied to air as late as 1872, in a passage about tetanus. "The exciting causes are, mental affections, taking cold, corrupt air, foreign bodies in the wound . . ." J. H. Pulte, M.D., *Homœopathic Domestic Physician* (Cincinnati, 1872), p. 51.

Line 43. How certain Ronsard's belief in witchcraft was, I am not sure. It seems doubtful that he would use this moment to pray against an emergency he did not believe in. His ode *Contre Denise Sorçiere*

(1550, L. I, 238), for all its dependence on classical sources, seems to include also bits of eyewitness experience.

Line 52. Ronsard's line, *"Force bleds, force vinées,"* means, "Plenty of wheat, plenty of vintage."

Lines 85–90. This is pretty much Ronsard's last word on the Age of Gold; to which may be added line 103—Keep idle men away from us.

Line 112. *holy gnawing flame.* Erysipelas. Saint Anthony's fire may have been an exaggerated form of this blistering, gangrenous disease. The ergot fungus, which poisoned stored cereals (and is the basis of LSD), seems to have produced this disease, or its effects, in epidemic proportions. Morris Bishop, *The Middle Ages* (New York, 1970), p. 255.

57. *Je n'ay plus que les os, un Schelette je semble*
Les Derniers Vers (1586)
L. XVIII-1, 177

Line 5. *Apollo and his son.* Apollo was the patron god of medicine; his son Æsculapius, a major practitioner in mythology.

58. *Meschantes nuicts d'hyver, nuicts filles de Cocyte*
Les Derniers Vers (1586)
L. XVIII-1, 177

Lines 1–4. Night is the daughter of The Earth and the Fates. Cocytus is one of the rivers of Hell. The sisters of Enceladus are the Furies, or Erinyes. Alecto, one of the Furies, has serpents in place of hair.

Amphitrite (Ronsard's line 5), daughter of Neptune, is sometimes considered as the sea itself (hence my first line) into which the sun is imagined to plunge.

59. *Il faut laisser maisons & vergers & Jardins*
Les Derniers Vers (1586)
L. XVIII-1, 180

Lines 7–8. Ronsard's lines mean, literally, "My pen flies to the sky to become one of the constellations / far from the worldly allurements that tempt the most wary."

60. A SON AME
Les Derniers Vers (1586)
L. XVIII-1, 182

Ronsard's translation, made during his last illness, of Hadrian's poem, *Animula blandula, vagula.*